THE NUMINOUS UNIVERSE

Daniel Liderbach

PAULIST PRESS
New York/Mahwah

The Publisher gratefully acknowledges The Hebrew University of Jerusalem, Israel, for permission to reprint material from Albert Einstein's work; and Methuen and Company for permission to quote excerpts from *Relativity: The Special and General Theory*. The scripture quotations are from the Revised Standard Version Bible, copyright © 1946, 1952, 1971 by the Division of Christian Education and the National Council of the Churches of Christ in the U.S.A., and are used by permission.

Library of Congress Cataloging-in-Publication Data

Liderbach, Daniel, 1941–
    The numinous universe / by Daniel Liderbach. p. cm.
    Includes index.
    ISBN 0-8091-3060-2 : $9.95
    1. Physics—Religious aspects—Christianity. 2. Presence of God. I.
    Title.
BL265.P4L53 1989
261.5'5—dc19   89-3151
                                             CIP

Published by Paulist Press
997 Macarthur Boulevard
Mahwah, NJ 07430

Printed and bound in the
United States of America

Contents

....

Dedicated to Karl Rahner
for the inspiration
and the example
that he offered

Foreword

....

As a physicist and as a priest I find *The Numinous Universe* both significant and stimulating.

Liderbach's objective is to analyze the openness of the "pioneers of modern physics to the possibility that there are dynamic presences within the world that had been wholly unknown to classical Newtonian physicists" and from that analysis to guide the search for the presence of God in the world of human experience.

It was the readiness of so many of the modern physicists to step beyond the "traditional wisdom" that enabled them to discover levels of reality that quite overthrew the ideas of the past. One is reminded of the words that Sherlock Holmes is quoted as saying, "My dear Watson, you see, but you do not observe." One can "see" in an accustomed framework; it is only when one is ready to change a viewing point that one can truly "observe."

This presentation is compelling and persuasive. It is only if you are open to new and differing experiences that you are able to appreciate the richness of the world in which you live and breathe and have your being.

I myself was born at a time when relativity theory was still new, and quantum theory was still under development. I started the study of physics when the fission of nuclei was just being investigated. By the time my graduate studies in physics were completed, the proliferation of "fundamental particles" was becoming a puzzle that seemed insoluble. Hence, my historical appreciation of Liderbach's presentation of special and general relativity and his analysis of the development of quantum physics is that of one who has watched most of it occur!

The presentation of relativity is superb. Particularly well done is the analysis of the world-view dilemmas faced by Einstein and the others who wrestled with the puzzling concepts of relative and absolute. I rather think any physicist would relish reading once more the development of the idea that the velocity of light is the same in any reference frame.

The author examines the attitude of Einstein toward the puzzling experimental situations. (It is, by the way, not at all clear that Einstein was aware of the Michelson-Morley interferometer experiment before he began his own analysis. But it makes no difference in terms of his freedom to investigate the velocity of light!) The openness of Einstein shows a freedom that is governed only by the world, not by any previously canonized ideas!

The same lesson is taught in the development of quantum theory. As a theologian, the author has not grasped accurately the complex ideas that entered into Max Planck's development of quantum radiation. However, the basic point is that Bohr, Born, Schroedinger, Heisenberg, and the others were open to a possibility that the world was vastly different from what they had previously thought.

A similar "openness" is what the kingdom of God demands of those who look about the world of consciousness and experience today. To discover *the presence* in the world demands a willingness to risk being faced with new and quite different challenges. It means "observing," not just "seeing" the world around us.

I have walked with many different people in their spiritual development. Hence, I am deeply aware of the difficulty in accepting whatever God wishes to present to us. To think of the kingdom as a definite reality today is often enough very comforting, but it is stifling nonetheless. Furthermore, to become aware that God deals with us through *symbol* is a great achievement for many. In the short run, symbols are less satisfactory than palpable and definite realities. But in the long run, it is in symbol that we find the world and God.

May all who have the enthusiasm to read this stimulating book find in it the expansion of mind and heart that it has brought to me. I trust they will be many.

James J. Ruddick, S.J.

A specialist in seismology, JAMES J. RUDDICK *earned his doctoral degree in physics from St. Louis University. Now an associate professor, he has been teaching physics and geology at Canisius College in Buffalo, N.Y., since 1957.*

Preface

....

The proclamation by the New Testament writers that the kingdom of God is in our midst signifies that within human experience God is present, actively offering invitations to humans to adopt new patterns of perceiving, of valuing, and of behaving in the world. This proclamation or kerygma summons humans to be ready to respond to these invitations by modifying their way of being human, rather than by continuing in learned ways. Thus, humans are receiving opportunities to develop along paths that they might overlook if they choose to retrace only the paths that reason and empiricism direct them to travel. God is opening paths through fields that reason might choose to avoid. The New Testament proclaims that God is offering these possibilities in order to allow persons to develop in those human directions that God proposes as enriching for human becoming.

However, persons of twentieth century culture in the west ask in their rationally critical approach to experience whether God can actually be offering such new opportunities of becoming human in the physical world. This critical approach could be a consequence of having adopted, either consciously or unconsciously, principles such as those of positivism.

Positivism assumes that the only valid method of knowing the conditions of the world and of discovering the paths to travel within experience is the method of empirical science; it goes on to assume that there are no forces and no presences in the world other than those that can be demonstrated by the empiricism of physical science. Those who adopt the principles of positivism can be tempted to go on to presume that the world as envisioned by the physical sciences and common sense is a mirror image of the world.

Consequently, some persons have endorsed the common-sense criterion for meaning—namely, that an assertion has significance only if it can be verified in sense experience.

However, because the kingdom of God does not appear within sense experience, such persons can conclude that there can be no harmonic integration between the proclamation of the kingdom of God in our midst and the scientific knowledge of the world.

Contemporary physics can here be introduced into this discussion in order to illumine the understanding of such persons. Physics of the twentieth century modifies the world-view of twentieth century persons by envisioning the physical world in a radically new manner. The world discovered in the research of contemporary physics is vastly different from the world as perceived by common sense. The physical world which contemporary physics researches is a domain in which there are more forces, dynamics, and occurrences than appear in the world of common sense. A significant difference between the world of common-sense knowledge and that of scientific knowledge is that the physical world studied by physics is a symbolic world that is inaccessible apart from the symbols of human imagination. The physical world discovered by contemporary physics is, indeed, the location of data that require a revised understanding of the world and, consequently, revised valuing within the world. The understanding of physical science has grown into a set of conceptual systems unknown prior to this century. This symbolic world of contemporary physics includes such startlingly new understandings that those who acknowledge this world might anticipate that the new comprehension of the physical world will lead to a new comprehension of human consciousness. This new understanding leads humans along paths that the reason and empiricism of common sense had previously ignored.

Thus, this essay moves back and forth between the evangelists' proclamation of the kingdom of God and the implications of the world-view available from the perspective of contemporary physics. The purpose of moving between these two poles is to demonstrate that there is a harmony between contemporary physics and the proclamation that the kingdom of God is in our midst. The thesis of the essay is that the kingdom of God is more convincingly present to those who assume the perspective assumed by contemporary physics than to those who assume the perspective of common-sense experience. The disposition toward experience that motivates contemporary physicists can profitably be imitated by Christians in their effort to discover a manner of practically responding to the proclamation of the kingdom of

God. Christians, no less than physicists, will be enriched by the approach to experience that is here to be developed, i.e., a choice to be open even to the dynamics of consciousness, even to the point of surrendering to those unexpected dynamics.

Those who claim special competence in the discipline of physics, as the present writer cannot, will likely find in the present study interpretations which they will judge to be less than precise. Such a weakness is quite likely to be found in any effort to work on the border between two specialized disciplines. Persons from one of these disciplines will find judgments made by a person of the other discipline unacceptable for authorities in the first area of competence. Similarly, those in the second discipline would criticize the judgments which are directed from the other side to the border that lies between the two areas. Therefore, there is a need to ask persons on both sides of the border to tolerate the lack of precision which will certainly appear at the boundary in the statements made by the persons on the other side of that boundary. Persons on both sides need to recognize that the reason for making judgments in border situations is in the hope of discovering new meanings in the interdisciplinary area where data can be interpreted by both disciplines.

A theologian engaged in an interdisciplinary study involving physics must presume that physicists will be able to tolerate the efforts, even the at times clumsy efforts, by a person trained in the verbal discipline of theology to reflect upon an unfamiliar object of study, i.e., physics.

The writer of this study is trained in systematic theology; he is reflecting upon data at the boundary between contemporary physics and the proclamation of the kindgom of God. At that boundary he has discovered a remarkable convergence between the intellectual attitudes and the moral motivations that emerge both from the work of those doing contemporary physics and from the writings of those who believe in the kingdom of God. Therefore, he has composed this manuscript, and he asks for a patient reading. But more especially he asks that the reader, especially the reader trained in physics, assess the efforts that are made in this study as explorations in an effort to find a bridge between the proclamation of the kingdom of God and the present culture whose judgments have been so largely influenced by science.

Thus this book is intended for persons who confess to be Christians and who cannot turn aside from an educated under-

standing of the world in confessing their faith. They can expect
to find in this book an understanding of the proclamation of
Jesus Christ for those who envision the world as suggested by
contemporary physics.

The author acknowledges the considerable assistance of aca-
demic colleagues trained in sacred scripture, theology, physics,
and the philosophy of science. Special recognition must be given
to Dennis Duling for his scriptural criticism, to Joseph Bracken
for his theological criticism, to William Nichols and James Ruddick for their criticism from the perspective of physics, and to
Joseph Clark for his philosophical criticism.

The assistance of Valerie F. Liderbach in proofreading was
invaluable.

Introduction
....

"The Kingdom of God is in your midst" (Mt 4:17; Lk 17:21).
That is the core of the kerygma of the New Testament. It
announced that God is present and active within human experience. However, if it accurately describes the context of human
life, then humans should be able to recognize within their lives
some confirming evidence that the kingdom is indeed present.

Thus, the present inquiry turns to contemporary physics in
order to situate the kingdom of God within the physical context
of human life.

Then it addresses data which suggests the presence of the
kingdom among us. The criteria for the presence of the kingdom
of God is found in the writings of the evangelists of the New Testament. With those criteria this inquiry can seek indications of the
kingdom of God that can be found in the circumstances of contemporary physics.

The face of scientific culture can appear to some persons in
present western culture as clearly manifest. These persons can
assume that they are aware of the general scope of scientific
knowledge and scientific method; they might, consequently,
assume that they comprehend the scientific criteria of knowledge
and the scientific method of judgment. This assumption can be
premature. Thus, as an aid to precision of thinking, this essay will
identify the criteria that contemporary physics has accepted for
its judgments. It will do so in order to confront the criteria that
might be used in a common-sense judgment concerning the kingdom of God with the criteria used in scientific judgments. The
intention of this consideration of criteria is to position the assent
to the kingdom of God within the actual scientific and cultural
field of judgment.

The field of judgment by the students of contemporary physics is a region marked with openness and an expansive vision.

1

Those same characteristics of judgment are needed by those who intend to make a judgment concerning the presence and activity of God in the world. Because students of contemporary physics manifest these characteristics of judgment, they can be taken as exemplary models for non-scientific persons not only in their judgments about the physical world, but also in the judgment of whether the kingdom is in the midst of the human community.

Consequently, the posture toward the world assumed by those who study contemporary physics will be an object of sustained focus in this inquiry. Their response to the demands made by relativity theory and quantum theory challenges those who are Christian believers to respond in a similar manner to the demands made by the proclamation of the kingdom of God.

An introductory reflection upon the world-view of contemporary physics here opens to the reflection upon the presence of God in the kingdom. Physics envisions the world as an interrelationship of new symbols, i.e., symbols which had not existed in the understanding of the world before relativity physics and quantum physics were developed. Consequently, the world that is considered now in terms of these symbols appears to suggest meanings of a world which is startlingly new.

The world envisioned by relativity physics and quantum physics will be focused upon as the scientific contribution to the reflection upon the kingdom. The treatment of this scientific world-view will be lengthy in order to allow this study to portray the scientific interpretation of the physical world—namely, a world of just such extraordinary occurrences as the world of the kingdom was proclaimed to be. The implications of the physical occurrences of the world, as understood by contemporary science, will be the foundation for the argument that there is a striking harmony between the kingdom of God as envisioned by the New Testament authors and the physical world.

After so focusing upon the physical context of the natural world, this inquiry turns to Jesus of Nazareth's proclamation of the kingdom of God.

Jesus' meaning of the kingdom of God can be discovered in the careful research of the texts by New Testament scholars. Norman Perrin was a New Testament scholar who had extensively researched the meaning of the kingdom of God in the gospels. Perrin's *Jesus and the Language of the Kingdom* integrates the scholarly work that has been done in the last century concerning the New Testament's meaning of the kingdom of God. Therefore, the present book has taken the results of Perrin's scholarship as the starting point in its reflection upon the kingdom of God.

Perrin's books, *The Kingdom of God in the Teaching of Jesus, Rediscovering the Teaching of Jesus,* and *Jesus and the Language of the Kingdom* reveal a range of methods of interpreting the meaning of the kingdom in Jesus' proclamation. In the first book Perrin researched the historical traditions from which the evangelists composed their writings concerned with the kingdom of God. In the second book Perrin researched the parables as his data for the interpretation of the meaning of the kingdom. In the third he interpreted the kingdom of God from the perspective of its symbolic presentation in the gospels. The subtitle of this final book, Symbol and Metaphor in New Testament Interpretation, suggests accurately the book's concern with hermeneutics, with textual criticism, and especially with the meaning of symbol. Perrin's focus upon the symbolic meaning of the kingdom of God reveals the flaw in interpretations of the kingdom that fail to acknowledge the symbolic character of the proclamation of the kingdom of God.

The evangelists' meaning of the kingdom of God will be placed in the present book face to face with the scientific values of the culture of the contemporary west. This will allow this book to ask whether the claim about the presence of the kingdom of God has any meaning in the present culture. It also provides a point of view to persons from which they can determine whether a confession of the presence of the kingdom of God is harmonious or dissonant with contemporary science. The question of harmony or dissonance will be answered by responding to scientific criteria for discovering meaning.

The hope motivating this study is that the reader will first appreciate that the data offered by physical science is harmonious with the world as envisioned by the proclamation that the kingdom of God is in the midst of the human community. This study also hopes that the scientific reflection upon the meaning of the physical world will make evident the need for a revised anthropology. This need is a consequence of that which anthropology intends to be. Anthropology is the interpretation of the manner in which human persons relate to the world. It ought to some extent be a consequence of what the world is, of how humans and the world interrelate, and of who human persons are. This latter identity of humans is partially a consequence of humans' knowledge of physical data. Moreover, the expanded knowledge of the physical world available from contemporary physics alters the manner in which humans relate to the world. This knowledge has been significantly modified by the efforts of physics to comprehend the data of the world that is found in occurrences within very small dimensions and at very high speeds. It has been modified, as well, by the enlarged vision of the occurrences and relationships within the world that contemporary physics has discovered. Both relativity theory and quantum physics reveal much that had not previously been known about the possible models for portraying the world. Physics, therefore, has revealed refinements in the self-understanding of human persons that suggest the need for a revised anthropology.

The focal center of this study, consequently, is the challenge to the reflective person to formulate the initial elements of an interpretation of human persons. Such an interpretation is the anthropology which is implied by the world-view of contemporary physics and by the presence in our midst of the kingdom of God. Therefore, the final section of this study will lay the foundation for such an anthropology.

If this general plan is kept in mind throughout the study, then the purpose of this book will not be obscured by the divergent poles of consideration about which it is to turn. The consideration of relativity physics, of quantum physics, and of the New Testament will converge to a world-view that is both Christian and harmonious with contemporary western culture.

Before commencing, the study offers a brief defense of the approach here taken to the kingdom of God and to the fashioning of an anthropology. This defense begins with a consideration of the task of theology. Thomas Aquinas in the thirteenth century identified the purpose of theology: "Christian theology also avails itself of human reasoning to illustrate the truths of faith, not to prove them."[1] Such, therefore, is the task that this study undertakes. It sets out not to prove, but to illustrate the significance of the kingdom of God by using human reason. It reflects upon the harmony between the kingdom and contemporary physics. Consequently, the context in which "human reasoning" takes place needs to be recognized as the milieu determining the meaning of the kingdom of God.

That context is present culture. In order to understand that context, persons need to respect the challenges, the demands, the assumptions, the values, and the judgmental criteria that culture endorses. If a person searching to understand the context has not shown such a respect for culture, then his concepts, or his system of thinking, or his standards by which meaning is fashioned will likely appear to be tailored for some other context, not for present culture.

This study, therefore, finds itself challenged to situate itself within present culture. It addresses contemporary western culture by an approach to the science that culture values. As a consequence, a relatively large portion of this study will be given over to developing those scientifically verified hypotheses which significantly determine knowledge in present western culture.

However, in order to avoid facile generalizations, the study intends to be precise about the culture which is the context for an anthropology. The culture of the west in the twentieth century has been profoundly influenced by the monumental advances in the physical sciences. These have had a profound effect in that they have transformed the manner in which humans grasp the meaning of the world. At the beginning of the twentieth century, western physics still used the seventeenth century Newtonian model of the natural world to interpret both the physical world and, by extension, all human experience. This model envisioned the universe as an exquisitely designed mechanism that operated according to elegant, deterministic laws of motion and cause. Science then understood itself to be challenged to analyze intellectually all the events in the universe as determined by these mechanistic laws that exercised universal and absolute authority. Analysis, therefore, appeared to be the principal manner of approaching any event or object of study. Conversely, synthesis, or the integration of events one with the other, appeared to be inappropriate.

However, late in the nineteenth century this Newtonian model had begun to appear to students of physics to be less and less appropriate as the path leading to the understanding of all physical occurrences within the physical world. Thus, in the first years of the twentieth century, some of these students began to explore alternate models of the physical world in hopes of explaining various enigmas that the Newtonian model had left unsolved.

One form explored as an alternate model of the physical world was a synthesis of the relativity of physical occurrences, one with the another; this displaced the model of the analysis of occurrences into their disparate causes. The hope was to integrate the complex interacting relationships of the physical world that had been passed over by the analysis of the world as a mechanism. Therefore, physics integrated the mutually interacting occurrences within the universe. These syntheses gradually became more important than the analyses of parts into causes. A physics of synthesis or relativity began to study the interrelationships of the seemingly spontaneous convergence of occurrences on every physical plane, even at the subatomic level. This preference for synthesis had become desirable because of the dawning awareness that the world was more like a living organism than like a mechanism, more a result of action-response dynamics than a product of a machine.[2] This shift to a synthesis of the physical occurrences of the world resulted in the physical sciences' becoming sciences of "organized complexity," rather than disciplined analyses of mechanisms.

This shift from the Newtonian model, which had permitted a clear, precise, and comprehensible vision of the universe, to the model of the organized relativity of the universe might appear to some persons to have been an unfortunate shift. The new model lacks the clarity and the comprehensibility of the older; however, it abounds in relationships which allow the human mind to explore previously unknown passages to meaning. The Newtonian model of the universe does not lead to the discovery of those passages. Those who prefer the Newtonian model turn aside from a perception of the world as a system of relativities; they direct their minds away from the passage that leads to a comprehension of the holism of the occurrences of the universe. They thus appear to isolate themselves from the world as it presents itself to human intelligence.

This essay has been composed, however, for those persons who prefer to reflect upon the world in terms of contemporary physics, who acknowledge that the universe is complex, who are prepared to allow it to present itself as an organism of interrelated occurrences, who anticipate that the ambiguity of the universe can be expected to emerge especially at those points where knowledge remains confronted with enigma and where comprehension of the world reveals interrelations of great complexity.

This essay envisions the material world as the relativity of physical occurrences within systems of organized complexity. It envisions the human world similarly as the relativity of human experience to the presence of the kingdom of God in our midst. It acknowledges that both of these systems need to be approached in the manner that they present themselves to human knowers, i.e., as systems that are, indeed, relativities.[3] It therefore proposes an anthropology that reflects both of these relativistic systems.

Just as the physical world is to be approached as an interrelating relativity of occurrences-and-responses, so too human culture can be approached. Such an approach to culture introduces a modified human self-understanding. If a person sympathetic with this essay were asked the meaning of the word "culture," he might respond by describing a complex of interrelationships that indicated a great many influences upon a people. Such a comprehension of culture is derived from the lattice of interpenetrating dynamics that contribute to what persons mean by "culture."

Thus, if a person hopes to address this culture with an adequate interpretation of its meaning, he needs to address culture as such a system of interpenetrating dynamics. It is the consequence of the integration of extraordinary numbers of values, behaviors, and understandings. Consequently, the interpretation of this integration must be couched in a synthesis that respects the organism that is addressed.

Hence, some consideration is required in this essay concerning at least one of the more influential dynamics that has been integrated into western culture. This dynamic within the complexity of culture is scientific knowledge. Because science has evolved along its twentieth century paths, persons in the scientifically oriented west prefer to seek meaning in empirical data and experiential verification, rather than in theoretical arguments. Therefore, western persons are encouraged by the physical sciences to test assertions by empirical experiments that demonstrate either a confirmation or a denial of assertions. Although this scientific criterion of judgment appears to support positivism's criterion of meaning, it is not to be identified with positivism's criterion. Physical science has discovered the invisible and insensible world that can be indicated only symbolically; positivism's criterion of judgment would acknowledge only the materially empirical elements of the world. Because of the fruitful applications of science to practical situations and because of the immensely successful technologies that have resulted, western persons have been conditioned to value not so much the sensibly verified judgments, but the clear, practical judgments that issue in pragmatic usage. Without such practical application or without the clarity that permits such usage, a judgment about meaning offers little relevant information to western persons.

Because of this conditioned preference for practical usage, the pendulum is shifting toward a holistic reflection upon the physical world. Scientists have come to recognize that there is limited value in an empiricism which stops short of discovering the non-sensuous relationships within the holism of the human context. Empiricism had sometimes ignored a comprehension of the whole human context. It had not addressed the complexity suggested by the entire range of the non-sensuous data available to physics.

Because of the importance of this synthetic model of the world, physical science is to be brought into the fashioning of an anthropology. Because of its synthetic model of the world and its holistic way of thinking, physics urges western culture to envision the world as more grand than the sum of its parts. The whole includes occurrences and dynamics that cannot be explained in terms of an analysis of the parts or of the separate occurrences within the whole. There needs to be, of course, a continuing effort to maintain the accustomed rigor and precision in the scientific approach. Today, however, physical science is fashioning integrated sets with which to comprehend the properties and relationships of its extended range of objects studied. Science is the model for western culture to expand its world-view by evaluating systems, not individual events.[4]

This shift in the method of scientific thinking is mirrored in thinking about the world that is not physical. An example of this shift is found in the thinking of a discipline distinct from physical science, the study of human nature. Today the systems view of the human person understands the person as interacting with his surrounding world. The reasoning behind this approach is that the person emerges from interactions within the world and expresses the attitudes and values formed from those interactions with the world. Thus, the person is not to be considered as a phenomenon that can be studied without regard to the system from which he emerges. There are, however, several worlds with which persons interact. These include the biological world that provides persons with their genes, the ecological world that supplies life support, the employment world that offers work to persons, the entertainment world that provides to persons situations in which to play, etc.

Persons, thus, are centers in which several systems converge in a concentric pattern of influences. Therefore, to understand human persons, it is necessary to study them in relation to those patterns of secular influences which form them.[5]

One of these patterned influences, physical science, has significantly conditioned persons of this culture. Many persons have been conditioned to expect to find answers to most questions concerning the meanings of the world. These questions range from inquiries concerning the propelling of rockets to inquiries concerning how parents transmit their personalities to their children. Physical science has also conditioned many persons to expect that the answers of physical science represent the closest that humans can come to a complete and certain knowledge about the world. This evaluation by some persons needs to be examined.

Quantum physics challenges those who so assume the complete knowledge of reality by physical science. Quantum physics needs to be treated in a chapter of its own, not in general terms, as this introduction would do. Nevertheless, at this point it might be appropriate to note that contemporary physics has discovered in its study of subatomic particles that it does not have what it considers to be a knowledge that is anywhere near to a complete knowledge of the world. On the contrary, it has learned that there are occurrences of the physical world which appear so completely to escape comprehension that these occurrences can be described neither by the conventional scientific understandings of the physical world nor by contemporary physics.

In attempting to describe subatomic occurrences, quantum physics has encountered various limitations in scientific knowledge. Because of these limitations, laypersons who assume that scientific knowledge is complete might be enriched by taking a careful look at knowledge fashioned by quantum physics. Any assumptions made by these persons concerning the objective certitude of the scientific knowledge about the world would, as a result of that look, have to be revised. One of the explicit intentions of this study is to lay out physics' acknowledged self-limitation in its comprehension of the physical world; then, as a consequence of this acknowledged limitation in knowledge, this study directs attention to the implications of this limitation for other forms of knowledge concerning the world.

Not only does physical science confess to its incomplete objective knowledge about the occurrences of the physical world, but its limitations in scientific knowledge direct persons to be aware that the subjective comprehension of the occurrences within the world is far from being as complete as some assume that scientific knowledge is.

Physical science is thus not ready to exclude precipitously the consideration of a presence, e.g., the presence of the kingdom of God, within the physical world; science will be shown to have grown chary about claiming to be capable of making a final judgment about the presences within the world.

Another limitation that determines the boundaries for the present essay is the clarification of the task of theology. Theology is charged with discovering the meaning of faith by proceeding from the known to the unknown. To proceed to the unknown signifies that theology strives to uncover meaning that had previously been at least partially covered or hidden. To proceed from the known signifies that the data which is used in fashioning meaning is drawn from the battery of data available to human knowers.

The present study proceeds from the known, i.e., the proclamation of the New Testament: "The kingdom of God is in your midst" (Mt 4:17; Mk 1:15; Lk 17:21). It then investigates the knowable meaning of this scriptural proclamation by turning to studies in New Testament hermeneutics. It next explores the implications of this for the present culture by considering the interpretation of the world that is offered by contemporary physics. This turn to physics is a consequence of the importance that present western culture has given to the interpretation of the world by physics. Those who choose to read this essay have nodded in agreement to the cultural importance of science. Such knowledge represents that which is known.

The subsequent aim of this study is to reflect upon this data. This reflection is intended to derive from the known a demonstrable relationship between the data of the New Testament and the data of physics. The reason for so proceeding is that the reader might thereby be able to discover in the relationship of contemporary physics to the New Testament a previously unknown harmony between the world-view of contemporary physics and the world-view of the kerygma of the New Testament announcing that the kingdom of God is present in our culture.

Then the reader who takes seriously the presence of the kingdom of God in the world will have before him extensive data for reflection. He can reflect whether a person can find in the world signs of the presence of the kingdom of God. Thus the study of the physical world is being brought into focus because its data can be reinterpreted to be a trace of the presence of the kingdom.

This book proposes to be cautious in its interpretation of such signs of the kingdom, i.e., it does not intend to "squeeze water from a stone." However, it does intend to assess the available data in order to determine to what extent this can be understood to indicate the presence of the kingdom.

The plan to be followed in this book is first to investigate meanings suggested by the physics of special relativity, next by that of general relativity, and then by that of the subatomic realm. The purpose is to discern what these disciplines indicate about the meaning of the physical dimension of the world in which human consciousness operates. Next, attention is turned to the meaning suggested by the New Testament proclamation of the kingdom of God. Finally, there will be two chapters that derive the world-view that is implied both by the kingdom of God and by contemporary physics.

1

....

New Presence in the World: Albert Einstein and Special Relativity

The kingdom of God is in our midst: God is both present within human experience and active there as king. Such is the meaning of the New Testament's proclamation that the kingdom of God is "in your midst." Moreover, God's active presence within the human community was proclaimed by the New Testament as having a consequence within human experience: God (the Presence) offers to human persons a wealth in choices of manners in which to become more human. That is the theme of this study, which presents the results of the effort to discover traces of the presence of God within the vision of the world that has been built up by contemporary physics. Hereafter this monograph will identify that presence of God within human life as the Presence.

However, the inquiry begins with a search into relativity physics for evidence of this wealth of choices within the physical world. Contemporary educated persons can take the kingdom of God seriously only if there is manifest within human experience some evidence of the kingdom. Thus, this study searches for the kind of new options for meaning that are implied by the proclamation that there is within the world an insensible Presence that makes a difference in human life. Hence, this monograph turns to the scientific study of the physical world; modern western persons respect science.

The culture of the western world often seeks to confirm its judgments with evidence found in data that are scientifically valid. Therefore, present western culture might be ready to acknowledge a judgment that there are new options for meanings of the world if physical science also acknowledges the evidence of such options.

The aim of the present chapter is to introduce scientific evidences that suggest that just such new options are available within the physical world. The method of demonstrating this is to argue that physical evidences suggest new, optional meanings for physicists; this is interpreted to imply that there are such new meanings also for those who intend to be responsive to the scientific evidences that call for new meanings of the world. Novel scientific meanings invite persons to venture toward the new horizons of meaning that such scientific evidence suggests.

A model of such openness to new meanings in a physicist is found in the young Albert Einstein and in his imaginative formulation of the physics of special relativity. The intention in beginning with Einstein and his special relativity physics is that this speciality of physics has made educated modern western culture aware that all meanings exist in a relativity to the frame of reference from which occurrences are observed. Consequently, every physical motion is assigned the meaning that is formulated by observers at a specific reference point.

Similarly, the Presence of the kingdom is assigned the meaning that is formulated by those sensitive believers who observe subtle evidences of "the Presence" from their specific points of reference. Such a point of reference is the posture of belief that the proclamation of the New Testament is to be reverenced. Thus, there are persons who locate the point of reference which trusts that the kingdom of God is in the midst of the human community. These can interpret the Presence to be active within experience because they exist in a relativity both to the New Testament proclamation of "the Presence" and to their experiences.

The younger Albert Einstein had been the paradigm of such venturesome vulnerability. As will be evident in this and the following chapter, Einstein was so disposed to be open to the physical world that he chose to proceed with a confidence in and self-surrender to the novel meanings that he could discover in the physical world. This confidence and self-surrender had been his personal response to novel meaning. He was able to sustain his research because of this continuing faith in his own research.

Einstein was born in Ulm, Germany on March 14, 1879 to a middle-class Swabian Jewish family. He was raised in Munich, where Albert showed himself to be an unexceptional child. In a culture which prized verbal memory, he demonstrated that he had a poor memory for words. However, he delighted in playing with spatial associations. For example, as a child he built card towers of great height; moreover, he loved jigsaw puzzles.

When he was four Albert's father gave him a magnetic compass, which he recalled seven decades later in his "Autobiograph-ical Notes." Then he remembered the wonder that this compass had inspired: it "did not at all fit into the nature of events which could find a place in the unconscious world of concepts. . . ."[1] He was, thus, already becoming aware that there were more ways in which to comprehend the world than he had initially thought.

Albert's mother and father encouraged their son's curiosity; they assured him that he could profoundly trust life in particular and the universe in general. Moreover, they gave Albert "the holy geometry book," a book of Euclid's geometry, when he was twelve. Euclid's work attracted Albert in its appeals not to author-ity or tradition, but to reason. Thereafter, he was accustomed to explore the possibilities that were latent within his own reason. This led him to become highly imaginative and inventive. For example, in 1896 he asked himself what would happen if he could catch up to a light ray and actually move at the speed of light. He was sure that the light wave would not, then, be moving relative to him, but it would, instead, be standing still. From that imagi-native idea the seed was planted which would grow into the spe-cial theory of relativity nine years later.[2]

However, in the interim his parents, in an effort to nurture Albert's inventive thinking, sent their son to a private (Catholic) elementary school. There he learned to nurture his imagination; he also became involved with the ritual and symbolism of religion. He wrote about this encounter with religion:

> (R)eligion (is) implanted into every child by way of the traditional education-machine. Thus I came—despite the fact that I was the son of entirely irreligious (Jewish) parents—to a deep religiosity, which however found an abrupt ending at the age of 12. Through the reading of popular scientific books I soon reached the conviction that much in the stories of the Bible could not be true. The consequence was a positively fanatic (orgy of) freethinking coupled with the impression that youth is intentionally being deceived by the state through lies; it was a crushing impression.
>
> It is quite clear to me that the religious paradise of youth, which was thus lost, was a first attempt to free myself from the chains of the "merely personal," from an existence which is dominated by wishes, hopes and primitive feelings. Out yonder there was this huge

world, which exists independently of us human beings
and which stands before us like a great, eternal riddle,
at least partially accessible to our inspection and thinking. The contemplation of this world beckoned like a lib-
eration, and I soon noticed that many a man whom I
had learned to esteem and to admire had found inner
freedom and security in devoted occupation with it. The
mental grasp of this extra-personal world within the
frame of the given possibilities swam as highest aim half
consciously and half unconsciously before my mind's
eye. Similarly motivated men of the present and of the
past, as well as the insights which they had achieved,
were the friends which could not be lost. The road to
this paradise was not as comfortable and alluring as the
road to the religious paradise; but it has proved itself as
trustworthy, and I have never regretted having chosen
it.[3]

Evidently, even at the age of twelve, Einstein had discovered
evidences within his human experience that there were far more
options available to human persons than either the conventional
wisdom of religion or even of culture had as yet imagined. He
had glimpsed evidence of the Presence.

The mature Einstein continued to discover experiences to
which he attributed his conversion from personal religion of conventional choice to the "cosmic religion" of the expanding
options within science; he recognized this conversion as having
changed him for the rest of his life. Thereafter, his bedrock faith
was the law of material reality as confirmed by scientific inquiry.
He had turned to the contemplation of the universe, a magnifi-
cent and orderly system that was, in his view, completely determined and independent of human will.

Such reflection upon the relation of the velocity of light to
the velocity of other objects set in motion his initial formulation
of his physics of special relativity. In a later effort to explain to
non-physicists this physics, he proposed a thought experiment.

I stand at the window of a railway carriage which is
travelling uniformly, and drop a stone on the embankment, without throwing it. Then disregarding the influence of the air resistance, I see the stone descend in a
straight line. A pedestrian who observes the misdeed

from the footpath (along the railway embankment) notices that the stone falls to earth in a parabolic curve. I now ask: do the "positions" traversed by the stone lie "in reality" on a straight line or on a parabola? Moreover, what is meant here by motion "in space"? In the first place, we entirely shun the vague word "space," of which, we must honestly acknowledge, we cannot form the slightest conception, and we replace it by "motion relative to a practically rigid body of reference." The positions relative to the body of reference (railway carriage or embankment) have already been defined. If instead of "body of reference" in this replacement we insert "system of co-ordinates," which is a useful idea for mathematical description, we are in a position to say: the stone traverses a straight line relative to a system of co-ordinates rigidly attached to the carriage, but relative to a system of co-ordinates rigidly attached to the ground (embankment) it describes a parabola. With the aid of this example it is clearly seen that there is no such thing as an independently existing trajectory, but only a trajectory relative to a particular body of reference.

Moreover, there is no universally applicable co-ordinate system or reference point from which all persons are able to describe the trajectory of the stone. There are only alternate points of reference, each of which is valid in its perspective relative to the trajectory of the stone.

Every description of motion is a relative point of reference; that which is observed from any point of reference can be accurately described only insofar as the observation is described in terms of the co-ordinate system of the frame of reference in relation to the motion of the co-ordinate system of the object that is observed.[4]

Thus, Einstein, as a youthful scientific theorist, had crossed the barrier into that dimension of human experience within which he had begun to perceive that there are more options for meanings of the physical world than conventional persons had previously imagined to exist. He had caught a glimpse of evidence that there is a wealth of meanings for interpreting human experience.

Those who find themselves in a relativity with the New Testament's point of reference are able to interpret this in relation to that referential framework. They might conclude that, according to the proclamation of the New Testament, the Presence is offering new meanings to persons. However, only those who find themselves at the point of reference which reverences the proclamation of the New Testament are in the framework that permits them to recognize that "the Presence" is thus active in human consciousness. Only such believers are in the appropriate relativity to the Presence as the interpretive meaning of consciousness.

From his perspective an option was available in imagining the self's traveling at the speed of light. He had envisioned that the physical forms of objects in motion at less than the speed of light would appear in altogether new forms. He was able to imagine, for example, that at speeds closer to the speed of light, objects are contracted in their spatial extensions.

Space Contracts

Temporal relationship was another example of this modification of form. When the coordinate system in which physical motion takes place moves at a velocity different from that of the speed of light of the observer, then the physical motion exhibits an inverse alteration of temporal duration. If the coordinate system of the observed motion increases in speed, then the physical motion slows down. However, if the coordinate system decreases in speed, then the physical motion requires less time to be completed.

Time Contracts

A third example was the relationship of simultaneity. Events which persons on the earth's surface observed as simultaneous he imaginatively observed from the speed of light as separated by temporal lapses. Events are simultaneous on condition that they are observed from systems of coordinates which move at the same speed as the events observed as simultaneous. When the velocity of any one of the observer-systems of coordinates is changed, then the events are no longer observed to be simultaneous. Thus, because of radical changes in motion, the perception of simultaneity can be modified. This can be comprehended in a thought experiment developed by Einstein.

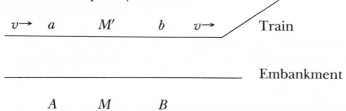

The experiment proposes that a person consider lightning to strike the rails on a railway at two places, *A* and *B*. The two bolts are asserted to have occurred simultaneously. If the two points *A* and *B* are connected by a line, then that line can be halved, i.e., *M* is the mid-point of *AB*. Two observers, one a passenger on the train at *M'* and one a pedestrian next to the train at *M* are at the mid-point of the line *AB*. The pedestrian, who is standing back from the track a good distance, can observe both places *A* and *B* at the same time.

The rays of light emitted at the points *A* and *B*, where the lightning occurs, can be observed from the mid-point *M* of the length *AB* of the embankment. Those points *A* and *B* correspond to *a* and *b* on the railway train. *M'* is the mid-point of the distance *ab* on the moving train.

Just when the flashes of lightning occur, this point *M'* naturally coincides with the point *M*; but with the train's velocity it moves away from that point.

The pedestrian next to, but at a distance from, the train at *M* would find that the flashes of lightning at *A* and *B* reach him simultaneously. But the passenger on the train at *M'* would be moving toward the beam of light coming from the point ahead of his position, i.e., from *B*. Moreover, he is moving away from the beam of light coming from *A*. Therefore, the passenger will see the light emitted from *B* earlier than he will see the light emitted from *A*. He will, thus, conclude that the lightning flash at *B* took place earlier than the lightning flash at *A*.

Therefore, it appears to the passenger at *M'* that the events are not simultaneous, though to the pedestrian at *M* the events so appear. Thus a system of reference (coordinate system) has its own particular measure of the time of occurrences at that point.

As this thought experiment demonstrates, there is no universal meaning in a statement about the simultaneity of an event. There is no absolute significance to a statement of time. Time is not independent of the state of motion of the body of reference. The perception of simultaneity which may be valid for two events as perceived from one coordinate system, e.g., by the pedestrian at a distance from the tracks, may be invalid as perceived from another coordinate system, e.g., by the passenger on the train.

The observer in the coordinate system that is moving more rapidly toward the observed occurrence will note the occurrence before the observer in the coordinate system that is moving less rapidly toward the observed occurrence.[5]

Relativity Dissolves Simultaneity

The reader might possibly conclude at this point that the concepts of time, space, and simultaneous physical relationship which common-sense wisdom or conventional wisdom generally accepts have been radically jolted by the extraordinary concepts of the past few pages. If such has been the case, then the discussion can continue. The purpose of setting before the reader the concepts of special relativity and of the reconceptualization of physical relationships is to lead the reader to appreciate that contemporary physics requires an openness to radical reconceptualization.

Einstein had, of course, initially comprehended the world with conventional concepts of time, space, and relativity. However, because he had been led first to put aside his a priori assumptions and then to adopt a radical openness about the observer's perception of the meaning of the physical world, he was able to fashion a new world view. This had occurred because he had been led by his research to allow his mind to open itself to that which it had not previously conceptualized. However, he could so reconceptualize only after he found a manner in which to free his imagination from conventional assumptions about motion. Fortunately, he discovered special relativity. The necessary requirement for the physics of special relativity was the willingness, first, to be open to a new world-view and then to be vulnerable enough to surrender previously accepted concepts of the meaning of the world and to accept the new vision of physical relationships.

With his openness and vulnerability to inversions of the meanings of the physical world, Einstein was able to glimpse that there are options for the meanings of the world. He had not gone on to inquire whether or not there might be an identifiable source for those options.

However, the present study proposes that such novel options for meanings within the physical world are consonant with those who stand in a posture of reverence for the New Testament's proclamation of the kingdom of God. These persons exist in a relativity to the New Testament's vision that God is presently active within the world, where God constantly offers to human persons a wealth of options of meanings with which they might interpret life. If persons were able to imitate Albert Einstein's openness and vulnerability to novel meanings, they would acknowledge their relativity to those novel meanings offered to them by the Presence.

A further model of Einstein's process in formulating novel options of meaning was his willingness to reconceptualize mass; he grasped that the mass of an object increases as the velocity of the object increases. Common sense assumes confidently that the mass of an object and the velocity of an object are independent. However, the increase in velocity of an object causes increments of the object's kinetic energy. Consequently, the object behaves differently because of this increment in its mass. Einstein concluded that the greater the velocity, the greater the kinetic energy and the more the mass.[6] This comprehension by the physics of special relativity was, indeed, another acceptance by Einstein of a novel revision of conventional meanings. However, more revisions followed.

One of these is the comprehension that time and space are not distinct from one another. Nothing can exist in space without existing in time. Conversely, nothing can exist in time without existing in space. The two measures need always to be acknowledged as influencing one another. Einstein inferred from this mutual influence that there is no such thing as space and no such thing as time; there is, rather, space–time. Space–time is a continuum which extends to every point in the universe. Nor can the segments of this space–time continuum be separated from one another. Every event and every person is located always in continuity with every other event and person in the space–time continuum.

Any object whatsoever located in space–time will after many

hundred years, i.e., after a change in "time," be identified at a different position in that continuum. The change of one element of the bi-polar continuum, e.g., the change in time, requires a correlative change in the other element of the continuum as well, i.e., a change in the spatial position. This bi-polar identification of space–time has come to be recognized as the continuum in which everything without exception exists.[7]

This critical revision of meaning in the physics of special relativity led Einstein to identify mass as energy.

In order to understand this revision, one might profitably recall the meaning of mass. Isaac Newton had proposed a relational definition: $F_{orce} = m_{ass} \times a_{cceleration}$, i.e., $F = m\,a$. An inertial mass, "m," is the constant of proportionality which relates the acceleration of a given body to the net external force of that body. A gravitational mass, also "m," on the other hand, is the characteristic of a body by which it is attracted to another body. Both meanings of mass are relational.

Einstein's remarkable discovery, however, is that energy, or E, is proportional to mass. The equation $E = mc^2$ expresses that proportionality. The constant of proportionality, the c^2, that identifies the energy in terms of the mass is the value of the speed of light squared. Thus, energy and mass have a proportionality identified by the constant c^2. This does not signify that mass might move at a velocity which is the square of the speed of light. However, c^2 is the constant of proportionality that identifies the energy that is in mass.

The revisionist meaning of this equation is, therefore, the mathematical relationship between the energy and the mass of a particle or of particles. Einstein proposed and then verified this relationship.

That which this chapter on "new world-relativity" brings to focus with this equation is Einstein's openness to a new and revisionist understanding of the physical world that special relativity revealed. Only because Einstein had been open to the possibility of discovering novel options and implications in the evidence which he was considering had he been able to discover this revision. He permitted the implications to lead him away from the univeralism of the Newtonian system in which he had placed his confidence and toward a revisionist comprehension of the material world.

Most significantly, however, Albert Einstein had been a paradigm for those who believe in the kingdom of God. He had imaginatively glanced beyond the range of vision of conventional wisdom; there he had glimpsed that there were novel options of meaning available to humans. Thus, he chose to embrace previously incomprehensible meanings regardless of the cost to him.

Those who believe in the kingdom are similarly able to glance beyond the range of vision of conventional wisdom. They too can embrace previously incomprehensible meanings. However, they can do so to the extent that they acknowledge that they exist in a relativity with the belief in the Presence. They therefore can expect the Presence to be offering novel options of meaning for the world. These believers need to imitate Einstein in embracing previously incomprehensible but presently appropriate meanings regardless of the cost to them.

These first considerations of the revisions involved in special relativity have served as an introduction to this demand for an openness to new meanings by believers.

The implications for the revised meanings of the physical world can now be expressed. There are two fundamental postulates upon which special relativity is grounded:

(1) The first postulate is that the laws of physics are the same, i.e., covariant, in all inertial systems; the mathemetical form of a physical law remains the same in all inertial systems;

(2) The second postulate is that the speed of light in a vacuum is a constant, is independent not only of the inertial system, but also of the source of the light, the observer, and the motion of the observer.[8]

The first postulate is necessary in order to salvage the theory of special relativity from the accusation that it has denied the laws of Newtonian physics. This first postulate implies a correspondence principle that is a completely reliable guide to the relating of the revision in physics to the older physics. A revision in physics, whatever its character or details, must reduce to the well-established classical theory to which it must correspond under the circumstances of the traditional theory that had been verified. The first postulate, therefore, insists that revisionist physics maintains the consistency which is expected of physical science. The laws of physics are the same or covariant.

However, there is a most important condition that is included in that postulate: "in all inertial systems." An "inertial system" is defined as a coordinate frame of reference within which the law of inertia obtains. In such a system an object is subject to no net external force. Thus, it is observed to move with a constant velocity. Of course, such a system can exist only in empty space, far from any mass. However, a reference system attached to the earth's surface is considered to approximate an inertial system since it has an acceleration only slightly more than a true inertial system. The external force acting upon the earth's surface is the small measure of the acceleration due to the earth's rotation about its axis.[9]

The significance for special relativity of the condition "in all inertial systems" is that objects in the inertial system of the earth's surface, e.g., a sensible object in motion, can thus be distinguished from other objects in systems upon which some more noticeable force acts, e.g., an object traveling in space. These objects, upon which major gravitational forces act, are then comprehended according to laws that need not apply to the objects fixed upon the earth's surface.

A significance of the second postulate, which attends to the constancy of the speed of light, is that it contradicts common sense. Moreover, it contradicts the Galilean transformations of classical Newtonian physics.

The Galilean transformations had measured the speed of any moving object by making allowance for the velocity of the observer who measures the velocity of the object.

However, the second postulate denies that the velocity of the observer determines even partially the measure of the speed of light. As difficult as it may be to imagine or to visualize how this postulate might correspond to common sense, which was a norm for the Galilean transformations, the uniformity of the measurement of the speed of light for observers at any velocity has been verified experimentally.[10] Moreover, the experimental evidence now available identifies the velocity of light as the upper limit of speed in the universe. Thus, only the measurement of light can be described univocally.

The photon, which is identified as the energy that moves at the speed of light, is observed by persons from any system of coordinates to be moving at a non-variant, constant speed. Therefore, photons are contracted neither spatially nor temporally, though all other moving objects can be so contracted. Consequently, photons are not comprehended by the physics of special relativity. Another way of saying the same thing is that everything which moves at a velocity slower than the speed of light is perceived relatively, i.e., everything except the photon is comprehended in terms of relativity.

Einstein formulated the significance of this postulate for the physics of special relativity as the measurement of mass — energy:

$$m = m_{(at\ rest)}/(1 - (v/c)^2)^{1/2},$$

where v is the speed of the object, and c is the speed of light.

The revisionist view, i.e., the openness to novel options of meaning, in this redefinition is that the mass of an object varies with its velocity.[11]

For example, if the velocity is 0, then the mass of the object is identified with its rest mass. However, as the velocity of the object approaches the speed of light, then the mass approaches infinity. The importance of the postulate is that it locates the measurement of all masses within a limited domain. Its definition of mass allows for measurable quantities. Nevertheless, there can be a less accurate measure of the mass of an object that moves at a velocity close to the speed of light.

This definition of mass in terms of velocity is analogous to the definition of space–time; the definition of mass in terms of evergy symbolizes the continuum in which everything physical occurs. Just as space–time identifies as united the two concepts of space and time, which had previously been considered to be distinct, so too mass–energy in Einstein's definition integrally relates mass and energy as convertible to each other. Yet the two concepts, mass and energy, had previously been considered to be distinct quantities. There had long been a law of the conservation of mass and a law of the conservation of energy.

However, after Einstein's demonstration of special relativity, these two laws were combined into the law of the conservation of mass–energy: the total amount of mass–energy in the universe has always been and will always be the same.

Nonetheless, this law of conservation of mass–energy applies only to the mass–energy that is found in frames of reference that move uniformly relative to one another. This limitation is to be noted as severe, since most movements in the universe are neither constant nor ideally smooth. Thus, it is important to reflect that the coordinate systems in which the great majority of mass–energy is located are generally not moving uniformly relative to one another.[12] Hence, the traditional laws of conservation are valid.

Nevertheless, Einstein's law of conservation is not to be discounted as trivial. He had discovered a genuinely novel meaning

for the physical world. Einstein posed his principle of relativity as
a reference point from which the conservation of mass–energy is
observable in those coordinate systems which do move uniformly
relative to one another. This principle asserts that, if there is a
mass, e.g., an airplane in flight, that is moving in a straight line
with respect to a coordinate system, then that mass will also be
moving in a straight line relative to some second coordinate system, e.g., a satellite in high earth orbit, removed from the first
system by perhaps a great distance. The phenomena, e.g., the airplane, observable from the reference point which is the first system obey the general laws of the second system as well.

With respect to these two systems, it therefore follows that
the law of conservation of mass–energy is valid.[13]

This principle provides a reference point for the velocity of
light, which is 300,000 km/sec. This velocity is a constant and
does not depend upon the velocity of the source of the light. Nor
does it depend upon the velocity of the coordinate systems from
which persons observe the velocity of light. These systems in relation to the velocity of light and to their individual motions move
uniformly with respect to one another. This is a consequence of
the second postulate—namely, the speed of light is a constant
and is independent of the inertial system, of the source, and of
the observer. Therefore, relative to the one absolute velocity, all
other velocities are relatively uniform. This follows from the
chasm that separates all other velocities from the velocity of light.
Thus, because the conservation of mass–energy applies to those
coordinate systems which move in relatively uniform velocities,
the law of conservation of mass–energy applies to the mass–
energy of the light emitted from all objects.[14] Einstein had discovered in this generalized law a meaning for the world that had
eluded physics previously; he had glimpsed in this novel meaning
something of the wealth of options for human living that is available to humans.

Before moving on to the consideration of the physics of general relativity, the essay pauses here to consider the distance that
has been traveled by this reflection upon the world-view of special
relativity. This distance can be estimated by considering first the
assumptions about the physical world which common-sense wisdom accepts. With this wisdom persons can become accustomed
to define the world to be that which it appears to the senses to
be. Thus, the fundamental notions of distance, time, and motion
are fashioned to accord with the experiences of the senses. These

notions of common sense have always been suitable for the worldly functions that persons perform in their experiences within the world. Therefore, many persons assume that their conceptions of the meaning of distance, time, and motion are the only correct concepts. Moreover, any concept which diverges from these conventional meanings is judged to be incorrect, or at least inadequate.

However, in the twentieth century physics has gained the competence to observe distances, times, and motions with precision and to analyze them with care. The result has been that the common sense definitions of distance, time, and motion have given way to highly sophisticated scientific definitions which diverge sharply from common sense. Albert Einstein's pioneering work in the theory of special relativity has allowed physics to formulate options of meaning previously unimagined, e.g., to observe that the lengths (distances) of objects that are moving at a velocity faster than the velocity of the observer are shortened. When this velocity approaches very great speeds, the shortening of lengths (distances) becomes noticeable.

Similarly, there is a lengthening of the measurement of the temporal duration of the motion of an object that is moving at a velocity slower than that of the observer. Thus, time moves more slowly when it is the measurement of the temporal duration of a slower moving object. This lengthening of time, however, becomes noticeable only when the observer is moving much faster than the object.[15]

In harmony with these unconventional changes in the measurement of distance and time is the change in the mass of an object that is moving at a velocity different from that of an observer. The mass of an object increases because of its increased motion. As an object approaches the speed of light, its mass increases to an inestimable degree.[16]

The importance of these modifications in measuring distances, in measuring temporal duration, and in identifying simultaneity can be focused by imagining that there are coordinate systems on other planets. Intelligent agents there, observing the same motions, distances, and times observed by persons on earth, would measure these in a manner quite quite different from that used by observers on earth.[17] Observers on Venus, for example, would be moving more rapidly than observers of earth; thus, by special relativity physics their measurements would have to differ from the slower moving observers on earth. Because the intelligent agents on Venus have the right to measure distances in the same universe as the intelligent observers on earth, and because their measurements can be valid, yet variant from earth measurements, there can be no such thing as absolute space or time that remains invariant for all observers everywhere.

Persons who are at different locations on earth, but who are in different co-ordinate systems, will, similarly, comprehend space–time in accord with observations from their own reference systems. They cannot comprehend these observations from a supposed, but non-existent, absolute point of reference. Neither they, nor any others, find themselves to be in such an absolute system. Nor can anyone even anticipate the precise variants in the measurement of occurrences by observers from points of reference in coordinate systems that are moving at alternative and unknown speeds.

Thus, space–time is observable only relatively. This is so in spite of the assumption that common sense might make, i.e., that there is an absolute measure of distance, time, and simultaneity. There are no reasons, except for those of common sense, that can defend the belief in absolute measurements of space and time.[18]

Observation of events is dependent upon or is relative to the system from which the observation is made. Einstein interpreted this to indicate both that space has been transformed into time and time into space. He therefore insisted that observers can appropriately measure events, distances, and durations only when they are located within the same coordinates of the continuum of space–time as the objects measured.[19]

To defend universal measurements of space–time by appealing to their separate measurements belies the physical relativity observable by those who apply sufficient rigor to their research of their measurements. Relativity would be weakened because the observed physical data would be removed from its actual relationship to the reference system from which it is observed.

Conversely, to defend the calculation of relativity by the use of the space–time continuum is to recognize that there are alternative coordinate systems from which occurrences are actually observed. Objectivity itself would thus be defensible as the relativity of space and time, one to the other.

To weaken the relativity of the physical world would even lead to a distortion in consciousness. This would lead to false, literal interpretations suggesting that the conventional assumptions about the world of human consciousness were valid. Conventional wisdom can erroneously assume that consciousness based upon sense perception is an accurate reflection of the occurrences within the world. Senses do not perceive the physics of special relativity; yet, that physics has been verified. Nonetheless, that physics, about which persons are not sensibly conscious, can rather easily be assumed not to exist.

This assumption appears immediately suspect when one considers that there are a great number of radio and television waves filling the environment in which westerners now find themselves. These waves are not sensed; nor do they become part of the content of consciousness, unless there is present a radio or television receiver in an activated state. Nevertheless, the waves remain a dynamic presence in the environment.

Believers in the Presence can easily take the step beyond the meanings of the imperceptible occurrences of special relativity physics and beyond the imperceptible radio and television waves in the environment. They can infer that there might indeed be other dynamics to which experiences exist in relativity.

The Presence in human consciousness, even though not detected by sense perception and thus not found in the content of consciousness, can be envisioned as partially determining the content of human consciousness.

To suggest that there might be such presences in our environment is to summon persons to be open to that which is unexpected and unforeseen in their experiences. To acknowledge the possibility of such presences is to note a caution, i.e., not to presume that the content of the environment is the same as the content of consciousness. Pre-formed expectations about the actual dynamics which operate within the world need to be examined. Persons have too often overlooked as fantasies the reports of subtle glimpses of such presences that acutely sensitive persons have experienced. Challenges to revise the understanding of the world are similar to the challenges arising from the once suspect research of contemporary physics. Physics has insisted that there are more options for meaning available to the human community than sense experience is able to perceive.

Culture is no longer able to ignore physics' evidence of special relativity, although relativity challenges the assumptions of classical physics about absolute space, absolute time, universal simultaneity, and universal objectivity.

Einstein's new world-view of relativity convincingly argues that all of the physical universe, the speed of light alone excepted, is relative. Thus, everything within the physical universe can be understood only from specific coordinate systems of reference. Particular coordinate systems determine significantly the content of consciousness. Persons consciously perceive physical extension to be modified by motion; so do they perceive durations, masses, and simultaneity. Quantified dimensions of the material universe are comprehended to be relative as they enter into human consciousness.

Contents of human consciousness initiated by "the Presence" might be presumed to be no less relativistic than the contents derived from the physical dimensions of the world.

For example, sense perception is determined to some extent by such identifiable, relativistic influences as persons' languages, ages, temperaments, environment, etc. However, there might very well be other influences upon perception and consciousness of which persons are not aware. Because of the possibility of such relativism, persons would be rash to assume that the options for the meanings of the world's dynamics are only as extensive as the actual contents of consciousness.

An illustration of the relativity of consciousness is that some venturesome persons' consciousness has been determined by their choosing the relativities consequent upon choosing to risk and to adventure in such experiences as interpersonal relationships or occupational challenges. Such choices determine consciousness to be relative to those dimensions of the environment that risk and adventure have introduced. Those dimensions would not be experienced by the person who has refused to experience such more fragile dimensions of the environment as risk and adventure might introduce. These two kinds of persons have quite different contents of consciousness because of their quite different attitudes toward their environment. The world view of each is clearly, therefore, relative to the attitude which each assumes. Their world view is not absolute or unconditioned.

The meanings of their environments, consequently, are relative. As the assumptions about and the attitudes toward our environment vary, the meanings which we discover vary. Persons thus can conclude that some of the meanings that they had assumed to be universally applicable are the results of subjective assumptions or relativities, not of rational and universal objectivity.

An example of a meaning that resulted from such an unexamined assumption might clarify the relativity in consciousness.

It had been assumed not only that the underground water in

Florida was potable, but that its value to humans was available only when it was above ground. Only then could people drink it. So the underground water was welled. However, after years of welling, an alternate value of the water became manifest. The underground water had had a value quite other than that of a potable water supply. The water in the earth had been a support for the surface of the earth. This value had been available to humans only when the water was underground. Unfortunately, however, the water had been welled. It had been removed from the location where it served humans as a critical earth support. Thus, the earth was caving into the voids created by the years of welling the water.

Persons have many such unexamined assumptions about the meanings of occurrences in their experiences. Some of these assumptions could be analogous to the assumption about the value of the underground water in Florida. The failure to examine that assumption resulted in a poor judgment; other such assumptions should not be buffered from examination. If an unexamined assumption is so buffered, then it is effectively treated as an objective absolute. Eventually persons might learn that their unexamined assumptions had foolishly been allowed to take on the absolute value of objectivity. That is a distortion in the basis for judgment that could lead to an error in practice. Floridians had interpreted their assumption to be objectively absolute: the only value of the water was its value as drink. They, therefore, welled it. They erred in practice. Large tracts of earth were lost in the craters that used to hold the water. Persons then learned that their assumptions had not been objective.

Clearly, freezing unexamined assumptions about meanings or values can be problematical in dealing with the environment. Similarly, to freeze unexamined assumptions about the content of consciousness can distort the world of meanings. Such assumptions, i.e., that presupposed meanings are objectively absolute, could be blocking the relativistic meanings of the contents of consciousness. The wise inquirer, therefore, remains open to alternative meanings and investigates the various options of meaning that people with different frames of reference might discover. The wise inquirer remains open, for example, to the relativity of the "Presence" to the contents of human consciousness.

Assumptions concerning the Presence of God within human experience enter the discussion at this point.

In the first four centuries of the Christian tradition, the Presence of God was a focus for worship. Christians had then developed liturgies, devotions, and rituals of worship that focused upon the Presence.

However, as later generations became more sensitive to human relations as a source of consciousness, their sensitivity to the Presence as such a source gradually declined. Liturgies, devotions, and rituals that focused upon the Presence had less value for worship, while communal charity, morality, and salvation were located at the focal center. Eventually the Presence came to be regarded by fewer persons as the source of the content of human consciousness.

Nevertheless, for some persons the Presence continues to be considered to be a principal cause for the content of human experience. As a result of these persons' trust in the causal influence of the Presence, they live with a hope that the Presence is leading the human community in its evolution. Such a trust in the activity of the Presence is found, for example, in the works of Pierre Teilhard de Chardin and Karl Rahner. These two have proposed that the Presence is active both at the root of and in the future of humanity. There at the root it initiated the process of discovering the many novel meanings that are available for human life. There in the future it summons persons to approach with trust the expanding number of options on the horizon of life that spread out before the human community. The Presence there invites persons to approach these options for meanings with a confidence that in them persons can discover conditions for life that allow human life to become better.

This vision of the activity of the Presence is in harmony with the world-view of the physics of special relativity. Special relativity has fashioned the world-view that any motion has meaning only in terms of a specific coordinate system which is its frame of reference.

Just as physical motion takes on alternate meanings depending upon the reference system from which it is perceived, so the meanings of the non-physical dynamics within human consciousness might very well be determined by the reference system from which they are glimpsed. These alternative meanings for human life can be accurate to the extent that they describe consciousness with consistency and rigor. They then would effectively expand the options for the meanings within consciousness. This expansion of available options would liberate persons to be able to live with the freshness that is the consequence of approaching life with a large magazine of options for response in the world.

Those who envision the Presence to be actively urging humans to move forward in discovering new options for meanings within the world might recognize that there is in the physics of special relativity an analogue to the many options available for the meanings of human experiences.

Some believers, for example, have chosen as their point of reference the option of regarding the world not only from the perspective of culture, but from that of faith as well. Thus, they have chosen to look at the world from a reference point that is an alternative to that which ignores the Presence. Their alternative reference point allows them to discover alternate meanings in experience. They have chosen to liberate themselves from the buffered perspective that is the consequence of refusing to adopt alternate perspectives.

These persons would urge others to be willing to open themselves to such alternate options for meaning and to the consequent fluidity in the development and evolution of the world. They recognize the value of pluralism in the options that have emerged from their alternative perspectives. Those who live with such a trust in the world's development under the guidance of the Presence respect openness to the fertility of the options in meanings that have been uncovered in such elusive dimensions of the world as faith in the Presence.

Before considering further the implications of special relativity for belief in the Presence, a brief history of the process by which Einstein discovered the physics of relativity is in order. This will reveal a paradigm of the intellectual attitude toward the world that allows a person to fashion a radically novel interpretation of the world, as Einstein fashioned his interpretation of the observation of motion.

The path to the discovery of special relativity had been discovered by the Michelson–Morley experiment of 1887. Einstein was confirmed by that experiment in his choice to take seriously not unexamined assumptions, but the need for hard evidence in endorsing the assumed meanings for the world. He accepted the conclusion of the Michelson–Morley experiment that there was no evidence for an ether. This led to inverting the meaning about the universal presence of ether in the world: there was no such ether, though the presence of ether had been considered to be self-evident to physicists.

In relation to the theme of the present essay, this openness to new options can be a paradigm for reflecting on whether there is any evidence for the Presence within the human community. If there is not, then persons can dismiss the claim by some that there is a Presence in the midst of every community. However, if there is some evidence of the Presence, then the reflective person can be as bold as Einstein and can conclude from the evidence that the assumption that there is no such Presence needs to be inverted.

This would be an inverse insight, i.e., humans can acknowledge a Presence that had been presumed to be absent. If there is, indeed, such evidence, then the supposed self-evident presumption which had refused to acknowledge numinous presences had misinterpreted the world.

Einstein had broken new ground in his response to the evidence of the Michelson–Morley experiment—namely, he concluded that the supposed self-evident presumption which refused to acknowledge empty space as able to propagate light was wrong. His ensuing inquiry concerning how light travels in spatial relationships with the temporal dynamics in a relativity with all observers demonstrated that the physical world is quite different from what common sense expects it to be—namely, distance contracts in special relativity, though distance is static for common sense. Similarly, time dilates in special relativity, though time is a universal measurement for common sense. Moreover, the common-sense simultaneity of occurrence does not apply to events observed from different frames of reference. The common-sense world and the world comprehended by special relativity are vastly different. Therefore, caution is to be exercised when common-sense presumptions about the world are posed. Persons should learn to mistrust not only the unexamined assumptions about the physical world, but those about the world of human consciousness as well. This caution is needed because the phenomena of the world of consciousness might be as far removed from common-sense presumptions as the phenomena of the physical world are removed from unexamined presumptions of common sense.

Human consciousness, like scientific knowledge, is relative to the points of reference of persons. In respecting the frames of reference that culturally different persons use, even if such frames of reference appear to be quite peculiar, reflective persons will not claim that the meanings that are determined by their own reference systems are to displace the meanings determined by the other frames of reference. Westerners use a frame of reference that identifies reason as the ultimate norm of judgment; easterners use a frame of reference that identifies spirit. The reflective person from either west or east will acknowledge that judgments made within the western frame of reference may not apply to the east, and conversely that the judgments made within the eastern frame of reference may not apply to the west.

More startling, however, are the subtle dynamics within human consciousness that are disclosed by the relativity of meaning within human consciousness. Persons who are unaware that meanings in other reference systems are as valid as their own will also be unaware of these subtle dynamics. Conversely, those who make allowances for meanings in alternate reference systems are quite aware that the meanings of human experience are subtle. Both meaning and consciousness shift from one reference point to another. Dynamics can be interpreted alternatively yet validly in different reference systems.

This reflection can appear to be rather abstract. The validity of various interpretations of experience might be clarified by an example.

In a personally experienced metaphysics class made up mostly of westerners at Indiana's West Baden College in the fall of 1962, there were two students from the subcontinent of India. Very early in the semester the teacher introduced as self-evident Aristotle's principle of non-contradiction: "The same attribute cannot at the same time belong and not belong to the same subject in the same respect."[20] All of the westerners accepted the principle of non-contradiction as, indeed, self-evident. However, the two students from India not only failed to grasp that the principle was self-evident; they perceived it to be self-evidently invalid.

However, that which is significant for the discussion of the relativity of meaning in different, human reference systems was the response of the teacher to the negative judgment by the two Asiatics. The teacher appeared to listen to their objection; however, he did not have enough respect for alternate systems of reference to accommodate himself to their perceived meaning. He did not present to the class a respect for the relativity of meaning that was manifest in the Asiatics' perception. On the contrary, he insisted that the westerners' perception was to be accepted as the validation of the principle. He might have recommended, but did not, that the westerners ponder the possible reasons for the tension between the Asians' response and their response. There was manifest in that tension the relativity and subtleness of meaning that are consequences of alternate systems of reference.

Albert Einstein would likely have called upon the westerners, as well as the Asians, to be aware that the persons from different cultures had had experiences that were valid for, but relative to, those cultures. He likely would have urged that each cultural group respect the validity of the experiences, the systems of reference, and the consequent interpretations of experiences by the other group. Moreover, he would have urged that both cultural groups go on to appreciate the relativity of the meaning of their own perceptions of experiences. This relativity of meaning might then, in 1962, have begun to emerge upon the horizon for both the Asians and the westerners.

The relativity of the meaning of experiences results, certainly, from the distinct reference systems in which different cultures find themselves. Thus, if the Asians had been westerners, they would have accepted the logical self-evidence of the principle. Conversely, if the westerners had been Asians, they would have balked at accepting the principle of non-contradiction. Yet, Einstein would likely have insisted that both cultures validly interpret experience. The Asian culture had just as much right to be aware of the ambiguity of experience as the westerners to be aware of the self-evidence of non-contradiction. The subtle dynamics of consciousness which are accepted by persons are relative to the culture in which persons interpret the experiences.

Moreover, in order for the western students to have appreciated genuinely the reference system that the Asians used, the westerners would have to have learned to interpret experience in the manner used by Asian culture. That modification in the manner of discerning would have required that the westerners recognize the subtlety of the relativity in meaning as observed from alternate reference systems. The westerners would need to become sensitive to perceptions that might appear to them to be rather elusive. Conversely, in order for the Asians to have appreciated the reference system that the westerners were using, they, too, would have needed to learn to become sensitive to perceptions which might have appeared to them as elusive. Generally, in order for any group of persons to appreciate alternate reference systems, that group would need to learn to perceive experiences within a reference system different from that which they had learned. Such a modification in perceiving would no doubt reveal the meaning of experience to be both subtle and relative.

However, if a person refuses to respect alternate reference systems for interpreting experience, then he is isolating himself within his own perspective. Such an isolating is, in effect, a claim that one's own perspective is a privileged and superior vantage in the interpretation of experiences. Such an isolating of oneself from alternate reference systems is, also, a denial that persons with different reference systems have the right alternately to interpret the meanings of experience.

However, not every physical occurrence is relative; one measurement has thus far manifested itself to be an absolute: the velocity of light. The motion of light occupies a privileged position among the many observable velocities in the universe.

Because the velocity of light is a unique dynamic in the physical universe, i.e., a physical dynamic that emerges as distinct from all other dynamics, then it does not appear to be irrational to hypothesize that that there could be similarly a unique and distinct dynamic within the world of human consciousness.

However, that implication is premature at this point. A premise needs first to be positioned: the premise of relativity, rather than that of absoluteness, is the general norm for comprehending meanings for the occurrences within human consciousness.

The motions, distances, and durations of the physical universe are comprehended in relative, not universal terms; the speed of light is the one exception. To the extent that the meaning of moving objects is determined by their measurement, to that extent it can be said that the meaning of physical objects is relative. Thus, meanings in the physical world are comprehended relativistically. Meanings change, as coordinate frames of reference vary in speed.

Meaning in the domain of human consciousness can similarly be comprehended to be relative. The frame of reference from which an experience is perceived determines the meaning of that experience. The earlier example of the tension between the Asian and the western students in the evaluation of the principle of non-contradiction is an example of this relativity of meaning determined by the perception of experience from different cultural reference systems.

The person who is sensitive to the possible implications of special relativity responds to human meaning in general with an awareness that all meanings may be relative. That person expects culturally determined consciousness to provide the framework that identifies the meanings of experiences. He expects, therefore, the meanings of human experiences to be relativized by the

frame of reference from which persons perceive. Meaning, therefore, as well as experience, is judged to be relative.

One variant frame of reference that judges meanings to be
non-relativistic is the coordinate system of positivism, which
acknowledges only the senses as the norm of judgment. Thus,
positivism rejects any meaning that cannot be verified in sense-
experience. This willingness to reject any meaning that arises
from any reference system that is not sensible is a non-relativistic
reference system.

A system which assents to relativistic belief is that which
assents to the Presence in all human experiences. This latter
frame of reference interprets all human experiences as having
meanings influenced by the Presence. Thus, there is here a relativism of God to experience that shades all meanings.

Such an interpretation of meaning is not dissimilar from the
hypothetical interpretation of geometric meanings that was proposed in the geometric vision of David Hilbert's non-Euclidean
geometry.

In 1900 Hilbert proposed that some of the axioms of Euclidean geometry be discarded in favor of creatively fashioned
axioms. For example, he discarded the axiom that through any
line there can be two or more lines which are parallel with one
another absolutely. In place of that, he proposed that parallel
lines intersect at infinity. After having discarded other axioms
and having added others, Hilbert developed a geometric world-
view for reflection that came to be known as Hilbert space. Persons who think in terms of Hilbert space need to modify significantly the meanings of geometry that had been learned in Euclidean geometry or common-sense geometry. Meaning in geometry,
thereafter, became clearly relative to the frame of reference from
which one considers objects, i.e., the Euclidean or the Hilbert
frame. Lines that are considered from the Euclidean frame can
be quite different from lines that are considered from the perspective of the Hilbert frame.

Similarly, the meanings of human experiences that are considered from the reference frame that envisions the Presence to
be active in all dimensions of human experience are significantly
different from the meanings considered from the positivist's reference frame. This frame of reference envisions every experience
to occur within kingdom space. Thus, the meanings of experience
are relative to the frame of reference which the person chooses
to use in perceiving. Moreover, no person's choice of a frame of
reference can be considered to be absolute or universal.

The person who interprets his experiences from the frame of reference that envisions the Presence in all experiences has accepted a reference system that can be identified as kingdom space. The person who interprets his experiences from the positivistic frame of reference has accepted that reference system identified as positivism. Both are relative.

The later chapter concerned with the Christian kerygma will set before the reader an interpretation of the kingdom of God proclaimed by the authors of the New Testament. The fundamental meaning of the kingdom of God is the presence of God in the midst of the human community. The New Testament authors exhorted their hearers and readers not only to be open to the revisions of meanings and values consequent upon the Presence, but also to be vulnerable to the consequences of these revisions, even to the point of endorsing social justice. Thus, the person who believes that the Presence is in the community and who lives with the attitudes that are derived from this belief is a person with a disposition to judge without regard for the criteria of the senses; this disposition is quite different from that of the positivist. This person's attitudes are also different from those of the person who unquestioningly embraces the technological and materialistic culture of the present-day west. The person in kingdom space has, in accepting the revisions of meanings and values derived from belief, located himself in a different "space."

Belief in the Presence provides a frame of reference which acknowledges the relativism of all meanings: it revises meanings in relation to "the Presence" within the world of human consciousness. In the world of human consciousness every meaning of any occurrence must be revised because it is perceived from the point of reference that is "kingdom space."

This chapter has addressed the relationship between the physics of special relativity and the Presence of God in human experience. The intent has been to present the manner in which the world-view of special relativity offers a perspective of the world that is in harmony with the world-view that envisions the kingdom of God to be in the midst of the human community. This world-view, drawn from the New Testament's proclamation, envisions the Presence to function actively within every human experience. The world-view of special relativity envisions every physical occurrence within the world to have that meaning which is observable from a particular, but optional, point of reference. Thus, the occurrences within the world reveal meanings to persons at one point of reference that those at a different point of reference cannot observe.

The implication for this study of the Presence is that there may indeed be evidences for God's presence and activity within the world. However, such evidences can be observed only by those who occupy a particular point of reference. Those who occupy a different reference point may not be able to observe those evidences. However, special relativity suggests that those who do not observe the evidences must not conclude that the evidences do not exist. On the contrary, special relativity insists that an observer at any point of reference recognize the legitimacy and the value of observations made from other points of reference. Persons at no one point of reference have the right to assume that their observations are the standards by which to judge the value of all other observations. Conversely, persons at every point of reference need to respect the value of observations available from other reference points. Thus, persons who may not be able to observe the evidences of the kingdom of God from their observations need to respect the validity of such evidence that is observed from other points of reference.

Relativity physics, nonetheless, remains thus only partial. Approximately a decade after his intuitive leap to relativity physics, Einstein made another leap of creative imagination to fashion the physics of general relativity. Thus, the present study turns to a reflection upon this wider relativity physics in the effort to discover a further harmony between the world of contemporary physics and the world in which the New Testament evangelists proclaim that the Presence is in the midst of the human community.

2

....

The Presence:
Albert Einstein and General Relativity

General relativity physics, not special relativity, was what Albert Einstein judged to be his greater contribution to contemporary physics. General relativity lays the foundation for an integrated vision of all occurrences within the universe. Its world-view is revisionist, even revolutionary in terms of the conceptual images that common sense employs in thinking of the universe. The present study turns to this revisionist general relativity in the hope that it will provide a stable bridge between modern culture and the kingdom.

The specific hope of this turning is to discover the extent to which the world-view of general relativity discovers within the world non-sensuous, but actual dimensions. The fundamental motivation is to surmise that those physical dimensions suggest the possibility that there are non-physical, non-sensuous dimensions of the world such as the world-view of kingdom-space proclaims. The divine presence in every experience was proclaimed by Jesus of Nazareth ("The kingdom of God is in your midst"). Such a non-sensual presence will be shown in this chapter to be not dissonant with the extraordinary, though hidden, physical dimensions of general relativity.

The general theory of relativity is not to be situated within the same conceptual scheme as special relativity. Rather, it goes beyond the limitations of special relativity. Special relativity restricts its concerns to the relationship between the motion of physical occurrences and the motion of those who observe occurrences. The more general theory is concerned not only with such restricted motions, but with all motion, even with non-uniform motion, i.e., with all possible frames of reference.

Einstein had discovered that an observer who is moving at a velocity which varies cannot distinguish between gravity and those

41

motions which also vary.[1] He used the term general relativity to identify his general description of any motion as it is related to any observer or any frame of reference. The relationship he described is not dependent upon the movement as perceived by the observer from the reference frame in which the motion or event is perceived.

This relationship between all, even non-uniform motions can be imagined in a thought experiment which can be conducted by imagining the experiences of a person riding in an elevator within an extraordinarily tall building.

This experiment begins with the elevator being first at rest. A man in the elevator car can be imagined to have no manner of obtaining information from outside of the car. While the elevator is at rest, the man can observe the strength of the gravitational field that operates upon objects in the elevator by dropping an object to the floor of the car. Whether he drops a key or a hand-kerchief, the strength of gravity is the same. Every object falls toward the floor at the same rate until its motion is stopped by the floor of the elevator car. The man might conclude that there is evidently some force, gravity, which operates upon everything in the car.

Then the car begins to ascend. The man in the car still cannot obtain information from outside of the car. However, he then observes a change in the force of gravity by again dropping objects to the floor of the car. The objects now fall to the floor more rapidly than they did previously. This can be explained by the reader by reflecting that the floor of the ascending car has begun to rise up to meet the objects that are falling. The man within the car notes that the objects now fall at a rate that does not appear to be controlled by the situation within the car, but by some force that operates upon the car externally. This appears so because, although there has been no change in the situation within the car, there has been a change in the rate of descent of the objects that were released. The objects are obeying the law of inertia, i.e., they are subject to no immediate force other than the force of the floor of the car. The floor now is rising up to meet the objects.

Unexpectedly, the cable of the elevator then breaks and the car, not equipped with an automatic safety device, falls freely in the gravitational field of the earth. In this new situation, the bodies that are released inside the car fall at the same rate as the falling car itself. They, therefore, are motionless relative to the car. The man inside the car, who still is unable to obtain information from outside of the car, could interpret this to indicate that there was no longer any motion of the car: everything within the car had become motionless. He might even interpret the new situation to indicate that the car had become an element within a system in which no external force, such as gravity, any longer operated upon objects within the car. In the new situation any released objects appeared to remain suspended in the air.[2]

The purpose of this thought experiment was to present an image that situates motion simultaneously within various frames of reference. Einstein intended to demonstrate that each frame of reference is equally suitable for a formulation of the law of gravity (and of the laws of nature).

Thus, within the frame of reference of the rapidly descending elevator car there was a meaning to gravity, though that meaning was very different from its meaning within a frame of reference outside of the building in which the elevator car was descending. Within the elevator car the meaning of gravity was that all released objects were motionless; outside the building the meaning of gravity was that all released objects fall at an acceleration of thirty-two feet per second.

Yet, each of these frames of reference provides a valid interpretation of the meaning of gravity, as different as these meanings are. This was interpreted by Einstein to be the principle of the equivalence of all reference frames.

For the purposes of comprehending and illustrating general relativity, the thought experiment needs to be carried further. If the man in the elevator car were somehow able to identify the precise physical direction in which the various objects fell within the car because of the accelerating force of the earth, he would have discovered that the lines of force converge. This would have indicated that the field surrounding the car must have had some external force or forces influencing the motions within the car. Thus there was operating within the car an external force that the man had not expected. If there had not been such a force, then the free bodies in the car would have descended along straight lines. However, they do not do so; they converge, however so slightly.[3]

Einstein's insight from this experiment led him to what he described as "the happiest thought of my life"—namely, the relativity of all motions, even non-uniform motions.

He had reasoned first from his thought experiment that

"there exists, during its (i.e., the elevator car's) fall, no gravitational field, at least not in its immediate vicinity." He imagined, therefore, that if it had been the man in the elevator who had been falling from the ceiling of the car, he would have been "at rest" in the falling car. He might have then, while "at rest" in the falling car, accidentally dropped an object from a pocket. This object, e.g., a match, "will remain relative to him in a state of rest, or in a state of uniform motion. . . . The observer is therefore justified in considering his state as one of 'rest.'"[4] The man falling in the elevator car, which itself is falling freely, would experience no objective evidence to indicate that either he or the objects in the car are influenced by a gravitational field.

Thus, within the elevator car there is no difference between the effect of gravity upon falling objects and the effect of the accelerating motion of the falling car on those objects. Gravity is, in this case, precisely equivalent to the accelerating motion of the car. This can be generalized: gravity is equivalent to non-uniform motion.

Relative to the hypothetical harmony between the kingdom and contemporary physics, there are indications of an unexpected harmony in this thought experiment—two forces, i.e., gravity and acceleration, have manifested themselves as together making up one force. Thus, though persons might assume that these dynamics are two distinct forces, they manifest themselves as integrated. This unexpected integration suggests that there are hidden dynamics, such as gravity, hidden within nature, such as the falling elevator car.

This first conclusion is the principle of equivalence, i.e., the equivalence of gravity and non-uniform motion. However, there was another thesis that Einstein fashioned from his thought experiment—namely, that gravity is geometry. The convergence of the lines of descent of the various objects in the falling car suggests that space is curved.

Just as space tells matter how to move, the matter in space tells space how to curve. The matter in the space of the solar system tells the objects there how to move. Thus, for example, the great mass of the sun influences the planets to move in gradually enlarged ellipses. Moreover, the great mass of the sun so influences the geometry of the solar system that the shortest distance between two points that any moving object follows, if there is no external force that alters its movement, is not a straight line, but a geodesic. A geodesic can be imagined to be an arc-form following the curvature of space–time. Such a definition strains the imagination. However, there doesn't appear to be a resolution for that strain upon the human imagination. The closest that humans have managed to approach to a resolution is by way of an analogy.

The analogy begins with two-dimensional configurations on the earth. These are non-curved figures, e.g., a cylinder or a cone. Though these configurations may seem to be not two-, but three-dimensional, they can be recognized as two-dimensional when they are unrolled onto a plane. Then, clearly, they fit onto the flat dimension of a plane. When they are so unrolled, they are no longer curved. The point of the analogy is that some two-dimensional figures do not appear to be such, i.e., the geometry of the common-sense world is quite different from that which it appears to be in some cases.

The next step in the analogy concerns three-dimensional configurations which are, indeed, curved, e.g., both the sphere and the hyperbolic-paraboloid, which is a saddle. The saddle is such that a person walking toward the origin in the XY plane would be ascending toward a peak, while, if one walked away from the origin, one would be descending into a recession.

Curvature, i.e., "Gaussian curvature," is determined by a mathematical formula: $K = 1/R_2 \times 1/R_1$, where K represents curvature and the two Rs represent the radii of some curved configuration. This Gaussian formula discerns that the curvature of a sphere is always positive, while that of the hyperbolic paraboloid or saddle is negative. Curvature in these easily imagined figures has been considered in order to allow the imagination to stay within three-dimensions. The point of the analogy is that the curvature of these two apparently similar figures from common sense, the sphere and the saddle, are contrary to one another. Thus, these apparently similar figures are actually quite dissimilar.

However, the analogy becomes rather too complex when it reflects upon how the curvature of the three-dimensional sphere influences the laws of two-dimensional figures traced upon the sphere. The common-sense rules of Euclidean geometry need to be suspended. They no longer apply to two-dimensional figures traced upon the three-dimensional sphere.

Euclid calculated the sum of the angles of a triangle to be equal to 180 degrees. However, any triangle traced upon a sphere would violate Euclid's laws for triangles.

A triangle could be formed, for example, on the sphere of the earth. If two of its sides meet at the geographic north pole of the earth and stretch to the equator of the sphere, then at the equator there will be two right angles, the sum of which is 180 degrees. Furthermore, there is still an arbitrary angle at the north pole. The addition of the degrees in that arbitrary angle to the 180 degrees formed by the two right angles is more than the total number of degrees that is possible in a Euclidean triangle. Clearly, the curvature of the sphere of the earth, or the curvature of any sphere, is so complex that it requires the common-sense laws of Euclidean geometry to be suspended. The curvature of a sphere indicates that there is a dimension within space, i.e., the dimension of the sphere, in which meaning is no longer the common-sense meaning of Euclidean geometry. The point of the analogy is, again, that the actual meaning of the world in which humans live is so complex that it is hidden from those humans who insist upon regarding the world with only common sense.

The analogy continues by considering the curvature of the more general, more complex three-dimensional space.

A vision of this general space can be constructed. Geodesics or curved lines of equal length can be extended from a point in all directions. The end points of all of these extended geodesics can be covered with a curved surface. The result will be something very much like a sphere, which is a three-dimensional figure. The area of a sphere can be calculated: $A = 4(\pi)r^2$.

The analogy repeats this procedure; however, this time the geodesics are extended farther by a certain distance. Again, the area of the resulting figure, resembling a sphere, can be calculated. It will, as might be expected, be a larger A. Then the procedure might be repeated a third time; again the geodesics can be extended yet farther. The A will again be larger.

However, after several repetitions of the procedure, the value of A will begin to decrease in its quantitative value, even as the extension of the geodesics is progressively lengthened. Eventually, the quantitative value of the A will be zero. The point for the analogy is that there are hidden meanings for dimensions of figures with which humans are familiar. Space can indeed be imagined to be curved; similarly, the shortest distance between two points could surely be an arc.

The analogy has addressed the complex and startling curvature of three-dimensional space. However, this has permitted the imagination still to remain within the space of experience.

However, the space–time of the physical world is a four-dimensional space, curved space. The human imagination, nonetheless, is able to fashion only those images that have been suggested by the experienced space that is three-dimensional.

The analogy thus needs to return to the earlier thought experiment of the elevator in order to indicate its implications concerning the hidden, unimaginable dimensions of the physical world. The convergence of the lines of descent of the objects falling in the elevator car can be interpreted to indicate not only that the center of the earth exercises a force of attraction upon falling objects, but also that the earth attracts objects along lines that are slightly curved. This curving of the lines of descent of the falling objects suggests that space, or, more precisely, space–time is curved.

Einstein had discovered the hidden, unimagined contours of real space: the mass of the earth, or any mass, warps space–time in the vicinity of the mass. This warping has been described as similar to the curvature of the surface of a rubber sheet when a weight is placed upon the surface of that sheet.[5]

As the rubber sheet in the vicinity of the weight, so space–time in the vicinity of any mass is curved. Consequently, objects that fall freely near the mass fall along the curvature of space, i.e., in geodesics. Geodesics are, thus, the shortest distances between the start of the fall and the finish of the fall of any object in space–time. Space–time tells freely falling objects to move along the contours of their environment.

However, if this extended analogy hopes to describe the curvature of real, four-dimensional space, i.e., our space–time environment, then it needs to locate this space in an embedding space or a space of more than four dimensions. However, the human imagination balks at such a task; it cannot imagine the curvature of four-dimensional space, much less that of space constituted by more than four dimensions. However, the incapacity to fashion images of four-dimensional space forces the analogy to be content to describe three-dimensional space. This space of common experience can be imagined to be the "embedding space" for space–time. Moreover, because of the contours of space–time, this "embedding space" is manifest as so complicated as to be puckered and warped.[6]

In order to discuss the warp of space–time, the analogy sets up an imagined coordinate system in which to discuss events in space–time. However, in this coordinate system, i.e., in the

"warped   cosmic   fluid,"   the   analogy   enters   unexpected
complexity.

Within this complex space the analogy acknowledges that the
proper distance between any two points defined by fixed values
changes with time.[7] This is radically different from the manner in
which common-sense space is imagined in terms of its distances
and the measurements of its distances. This "warped" curvature
of space–time is a form of space very different from the form of
space in which humans confidently locate themselves as living.
Moreover, because humans cannot step outside of real space to
look at this warped space from the outside, as they can look at a
sphere or a saddle, they can neither envision nor imagine the curvature of space–time.

They can, however, derive some slight appreciation of that
curvature from the properties used to describe it.[8] One such
property is discovered from observing the direction of beams of
light within space–time; these can be observed to converge in real
space. Thus, space–time apparently curves in upon itself. This
convergence of lines within space–time converges with the
motion of all bodies moving in real space, such as the falling
objects in the elevator car. Those bodies, as well as all bodies,
move through space–time not in straight lines, but in geodesics,
the straightest lines in space–time. This coincides with the observation of beams of light which move, as all bodies move, as space–
time dictates, i.e., not in straight, but in curved lines.

The analogy between four-dimensional space–time and
three-dimensional images of that unimaginable framework can be
here brought to closure. The purpose of the analogy was to provide some indication of the hidden dimensions of the physical
world, its complexity, and its enigmatic configuration. This has
been done by an analogy. If the contours of the more simple
three-dimensional "embedding" space are so complex as to force
the human imagination to stretch to its limits in envisioning, then
the more complex four-dimensional space–time must be even
more distantly removed from that which the human imagination
can envision.

This hypothesis of the contours of space–time could be and
had been quite strenuously rejected. However, an experimental
verification of Einstein's hypothesis of the curvature of space–
time was conducted by Einstein beginning on May 29, 1919, after
a total eclipse of the sun.

During the eclipse, the stars which are in line both with the earth and with the eclipsed sun become visible in the darkness surrounding the eclipsed sun. The beams of light from those distant stars behind the sun had to pass very close to the edge of the sun; they then bent in the curved space around the sun. This bending could be observed by comparing photographs of the light from those stars taken at the time of the eclipse with photographs taken six months later. After six months, the sun is no longer near the light path of these stars, as it had been at the time of the eclipse. In the later photographs the stars had appeared to have shifted in their celestial position. Einstein explained this to have resulted not from a shift in position, but from the prior bending of their beams of light in their passage through the curved space–time around the sun during the eclipse. Thus, the curvature of space–time had been verified.[9]

In harmony with this verified curvature of real space–time, the orbits of the planets of the solar system are ellipses, not circles: ellipses are curved, while circles are not. The planets, as all objects in space–time, are directed by space–time to move along the contours of curved or warped celestial curvature.[10]

Also in harmony with this verified curvature, gravity has been identified as a form of geometry. The geometry of space–time, i.e., the framework in which objects move, is distorted by the great pieces of matter in that framework. Thus, space–time is markedly warped in the vicinity of these pieces of matter, especially near such large masses as stars. Consequently, just as a navigator of the oceans needs to comprehend the spherical trigonometry of the coordinate system of earth in order to navigate on the globe, so too the geophysicist needs to know the geometric curvature of space–time near masses in order to comprehend the motions of objects in the curvature of space–time.

Einstein's hypothesis had discarded the theory that gravity is the attractive force of large bodies; this had been the interpretation of gravity that was proposed by Isaac Newton.

Rather, gravity is the curvature of the space–time continuum in the neighborhood of large masses.[11] Therefore, space vehicles need to account not for the force of attraction of large pieces of matter, but for the geometry of the contours of the space–time in the neighborhood of those masses near which the space vehicles are to move.[12]

Furthermore, the pulsations of the universe are explained by this geometry. The universe expands and contracts because of the directives that it receives from its curvature.

The telescopically observed reddening of distant stars has been interpreted to be a consequence of pulsation; the pulsation is caused by a warped universe. The red appearance of a star is understood to indicate that the star is receding. This can be observed in one of the nearest clouds of stars Andromeda Nebula which manifests a .05% reddening. This reddening can also be observed in nebulae of stars which are located at the limit distance of present telescopic powers; these nebulae manifest a reddening of approximately 15%. These observations suggest that the universe is presently in the expansion cycle of its pulsation.

However, because of the curvature of space–time, this expansion must eventually fold in upon itself as it follows the warp of space–time. Then a contraction will begin when the expansion warps along the curvature. That later expansion into that curvature will cause the space–time continuum to become dense, i.e., warped in the neighborhood of great masses. As a result of this density, there will be a contraction along the dialectic balance in the continuum of the universe.[13]

The intellectual mind-set toward the world that is suggested by this perspective of general relativity physics reveals latent meanings for the world: there are actual dimensions of the universe that remain hidden from human perceptions by common sense.

The meaning of the universe and the vision of space–time that have been posed by the physics of general relativity thus summon humans away from their prior visions of the universe. In place of the assumption that the frame of reference of space is a rectangluar coordinate system which is similar to a container of immeasurable dimensions, curved space–time is positioned as the universal frame of reference. This space–time continuum expands and contracts. Such would be unthinkable if the universe were analogous to an immense container.

Furthermore, the revisionist vision of general relativity is, if not unthinkable, certainly unimaginable. Human images can be drawn only from the world of three dimensions; thus, images of the plurality of dimensions of the space–time continuum are not at hand.

Nevertheless, the unimaginable reference frame of space–time does invite humans to rethink their meanings for the reference frame in which they live. The space–time in which life is embedded is so enigmatically complex that its comprehension has been moved beyond the ordinary and into the extraordinary. The dimensions of the universe are enigmas that are beyond the power of human imagination to analyze or even to envision. They demand that new meanings for the world be fashioned. These new meanings could well extend to a presence within the universe of a personal dynamic similar to that which had been proclaimed by the New Testament authors: the active presence of God.

The new interpretations suggested, but not implied, by general relativity allow the human mind to contemplate unexpected conceptualizations, such as the Presence. This can be imagined, but not comprehended.

We have learned from this brief reflection upon the curvature of space–time that common sense assumptions about space can distort space–time.

Similarly, common sense may have distorted the meanings of the world of human consciousness. We can formulate more accurately an understanding of our spatial and temporal frame of reference only by remaining open to the enigmatic contours of the geometry of warped space–time.

So we may need to remain open to similarly enigmatic revelations of new meanings and new options for meanings within the domain of consciousness. This domain might include dimensions beyond the powers of the human imagination to envision, just as the curvature of space–time's geometry studied by general relativity is beyond human images. Human comprehension of the more familiar, physical dimensions of the space of the world have been modified to reflect the contours of space–time. Human comprehension, therefore, and human images of the world of consciousness will similarly likely need to be modified.

An example of such a transformation through the modification of images might be helpful.

Persons not familiar with the geographical contours of the land mass upon which Pittsburgh, Pennsylvania is built are likely to find driving an automobile there to be quite difficult without carefully following a map. The city is warped, to borrow the language of general relativity, by the large mass upon which it is built. Streets that appear to be straight are arched.

The domain of human consciousness might similarly be fashioned according to hidden contours that alter apparently familiar domains into dimensions that can be entered properly only after having adopted new meanings and new options.

If, for example, there is within the world of consciousness a Presence who influences all experiences, then the human world, too, has unexpected contours that need to be taken into consideration.

The kingdom of God in the midst of the human community then functions very like the large masses in space–time, or the large mass upon which Pittsburgh is built. Just as large masses tell objects how to move when these objects are in the neighborhood of the masses, so too some hidden force might curve or "warp" its surrounding environment and thus influence certain events to occur within human experience. For example, one can ponder the source of the heroic act, of the choice to be unnecessarily vulnerable, or of the risk of genuine freedom. If the Presence is the source of such events (such is not less extraordinary than the curvature of space–time), then persons need to make allowances for these hidden contours of human consciousness influenced by the Presence. Otherwise they will not be able to orient themselves to the events that they experience.

The world of consciousness may, indeed, be profoundly different from what common sense assumes. However, the description of how the domain of human consciousness might be different from its appearances is unavailable.

Only in the twentieth century has the description of a revision of physical space–time become accessible. That imaginative world-view emerged with Albert Einstein's general theory of relativity in 1915–16.

Since then the community of physicists has been working to develop the implication of Einstein's physics: a unified field theory of electricity, quantum physics, and gravity. Sheldon Lee Glashow and Howard Georgi have taken up the unfinished research of Kaluza and Weyl on this frontier of human knowledge. They are seeking to discover a method of describing the hidden contours of the physical universe in hopes of integrating all forces within one field. As their work proceeds, humans need to remain open to a revision in the description of the conventional meaning of the frame of reference that is the familiar, human, physical living space.

The goal of this research into a unified field theory has been to describe the physical world in terms that integrate all interactions, sensuous and non-sensuous, which propagate through space. Electromagmetic interactions, gravitational interactions, and quantum interactions form parts of such a unified theory. However, thus far, the scientific community has been unable to settle upon a reasonably satisfying description of the universe.

The so-called second quantization of matter has forced repeated revisions of the field theories which have been suggested.

Furthermore, as science, probing into the fundamentals of material reality, discovers more and more elementary forms of matter, the possibility of settling upon a permanent and integrative description of the physical universe has appeared to become elusive. However, this will be considered in the following chapter.

The reason for considering the efforts toward a unified field theory at this point is to bring into focus the challenge set before all persons to remain open to revisions in the meaning not only of the physical universe, but also of human consciousness. The vision of the universe of general relativity physics certainly calls forth the possibility that there might be within the world of human consciousness dynamics and possibilities that sense perception and common sense have not perceived.

If research into the physical universe has suggested a revision of the meaning of the universe, then it appears at least as reasonable to assume that research into the world of human consciousness will require a description that similarly revises meaning.

Insofar as human intercommunication occurs largely because of complex human minds' interacting and interpenetrating, to that extent persons must expect the world of human consciousness to be increasingly complex. Furthermore, just as there is as yet no satisfactory description of the physical universe, no unified field theory, so, too, there is as yet no completely adequate description of the constitution of the world of consciousness. There is no exhaustively adequate description of physical occurrences, nor of human experiences, nor of the possible influence of the Presence in the world. Just as the description of the physical universe requires that humans stretch their powers of imagination in order to comprehend, so, too, the tentative description of the influence of the Presence upon the world of human consciousness requires a stretching of the imagination. Just as the description of the physical universe has indicated that the material world is far more complex and more holistically interpenetrating than we had assumed, so, too, the domain of human consciousness will likely require a descriptive context that includes more influences, such as the Presence, which penetrate consciousness than humans had previously imagined.

Let one imagine that the choice to risk a freely chosen venture into an unknown future is influenced by the Presence. This stretching of the imagination might be more than some persons are willing to entertain because the tentatively proposed images for that world might appear to be revolutionary. However, general relativity proposes revolutionary images of a pulsating universe, a universe curved in upon itself, the geodesic rather than the straight line as the shortest distance between two points, and the area of a sphere first expanding and then contracting as its radii are extended are all certainly revolutionary images. The physical universe in which we live is, indeed, a space–time that eludes any human effort at visualization. It can be described only in the revisionist images of physics. If these images were rejected because of their revolutionary character, then we would be much further from appreciating the actual, present reference frame for the world. It would be crippling to reject interpretations that are revisionist simply because they are revolutionary. The questions to be asked of a reinterpretation are whether its images contribute to a description of the data in question and whether an argument supports the reinterpretation. If the images do so contribute and are so supported, then the images deserve to be given a respectful place in the imagination.

Indeed, the reinterpretation of the world of human consciousness as occurring within the reference frame in which the Presence of God is active within the human community is revisionist and revolutionary. Nonetheless, arguments will be offered in this essay to defend this reinterpretation of human consciousness. That revision will be presented as deserving a respectful place in the imagination.

The argument thus far presented has been a demonstration that general relativity physics has revised the meaning of the physical universe. The argument also considered the implications that might be inferred from these revisions. One of these inferred implications has been that the world of human consciousness is at least as complex, as interpenetrated by the extraordinary, and as enigmatic as the domain of the physical universe has been scientifically interpreted to be.

A cautionary note might well be introduced at this point. There is a problem in the physics of general relativity in that its synthetic proposal for the meaning of empirical data is unimaginable. The proposal that the Presence is in the midst of the human community similarly synthesizes a world-view that is beyond imagination. The claim that the Presence is found in the midst of the community can be expected to be countered by the common sense demand for a concrete, explanatory image of such Presence. In the absence of that image, common sense will likely refuse to accept the interpretation that the Presence is actively functioning.

A response to this refusal would be first to recognize that contemporary physics seeks not to explain the universe, but to describe. Next one might respond by appealing to the value of seeking not for images or visual representations of the Presence, but for traces of evidence that there is such a Presence within human consciousness. Just as physics has discovered new options for understanding the world from the subtle traces of occurrences that are non-sensible, so reflection upon consciounsess might be able to discover within the world new options for meaning and choice from subtle traces within consciousness of occurrences that might not be sensible. Yet, where can this evidence can be found? Where might these subtle traces of the Presence manifest themselves within consciousness? Where is there evidence of a hope that is unseen and imageless?

The evidence of such a horizon can be found in the actual options that have been made by some persons. Some persons are obviously conscious of an expansive Presence whose influence emerges from their actually chosen interpretations. Many of these options manifest themselves as unique insofar as they reveal that the persons choosing have drastically revised their human values and choices.

For example, there are victims of injustice who choose to remain quiet, even though they might have chosen to defend themselves from being treated unjustly. Those who have encountered such persons are aware that these persons are extraordinary in their willingness to be vulnerable. They present in their vulnerability evidence of a force within their lives that is not sensible. Some force has motivated them to remain open, though they need not be so. This unsensed force has invited these persons to revise their choices and to choose new options for living. There is in those persons a dynamic of hope operating within their choices. The vulnerable person hopes that human life will be better for everyone if persons are open and vulnerable to one another. However, this hope is a consequence not of reasoning, but of a dynamic that is neither sensible nor the result of common sense.

This identification of evidences of the transcendent dynamic within such human options was done by Karl Rahner. He identified other such evidences of the Presence within human consciousness.

He identified another trace of the Presence in persons who

forgive those who offend them, though these offenders take the forgiveness for granted. The forgiving persons choose to be merciful because of the value of mercy.

Similarly, there are persons who obey an interior call which they identify as the call of God. They respond to a mysterious, silent, incomprehensible Presence who voicelessly invites them to do that which they would not otherwise do. They respond without considering how costly their response might be in terms of revising the patterns of their lives. These responses indicate the presence of a dynamic within human experience and human consciousness that is powerful enough to influence human consciousness, yet that is beyond images and beyond sensible experiences. This Presence motivates persons to respond to it, although their response earns for them no material advantages. This is a response to choose those new options for living offered by the Presence.

These choices are traces of a non-sensible Presence that signifies new horizons of hope.

Still other traces of the Presence within human experiences have been identified by Rahner. He has directed attention to many human experiences that indicate the choice of extraordinary options of values for life within the world. He directs attention to those persons who have generously given their valued possessions or positions to persons who are in need of these, though the recipients fail to express either thanks or recognition. Some will at times make such sacrifices even without an interior feeling of satisfaction. They, thus, may be allowing themselves to experience an absolute loneliness. The implications of the choice to be so generous, even at the cost of loneliness and of receiving no thanks, are monumental. These choices imply a judgment based upon conscience; the Presence in conscience leads persons so to respond.

Some persons strive to reply to the urgings of their conscience in order to respond faithfully to the silent God who may long ago have ceased to comfort them for their fidelity, the God who can appear to turn a deaf ear to their prayer and who can seem to have removed himself from them to the opposite side of a limitless abyss.

There are persons, as well, whose behavior is motivated by their personal choice of a value that has demanded their surrender of their own personal security. These persons can appear to others to be obliterating themselves.

These experiences of an interior dynamic are explainable not in terms of the material world. These experiences are not consequences of calculated rewards that can be accrued. Rather, they are responses to an interior dynamic that eludes material identification. More positively, these are traces of that dynamic within consciousness that can be identified as the Presence.[14]

Moreover, three historical evidences of this Presence can be cited to confirm that there are traces of the Presence perceived by specific personalities. Albert Camus, Anne Frank and Robert Bolt acted in response to an interior dynamic that eludes an empirical identification, but that offered to them options of revised values.

Albert Camus had befriended a young German while the two were in northern Africa. They had agreed that because of the incongruity and perhaps the absurdity of life, persons are free to do that which they discern to be humanly dignified. However, the criteria for discerning dignity are ambiguous; there do not seem to be intellectually based criteria by which persons are to access their choices.

However, a few years later Camus learned that the German had become a member of the Waffen SS in Hitler's Third Reich. He wrote to his friend in order to reproach him for ignoring the human criteria not of the intelligence, but of the spirit. The criteria of intelligence may be ignored, but not those of the spirit. According to the spirit's summons, there are certain choices that persons may not make. They are not free to assume the right to kill men, even if the failure to kill might lead to humiliation and defeat.[15]

The incongruity or absurdity of life does not give persons a justification for ignoring the interior dynamic that they find to be active within their spirits. Camus insisted with his friend that he should have attended to this dynamic, whether or not he found it to be attractive.

This study, as well as any Christian believer, might identify that dynamic to be the Presence who was actively influencing Albert Camus from within his personal experience.

Anne Frank's diary during her two years of seclusion (1943–1945) within the Third Reich's Amsterdam is a second historical record of the traces of the Presence within the world. Anne was aware that members of the Jewish community were being taken away; she was also aware that among the Jews of Amsterdam the degree of confidence in life was gradually diminishing. Yet, the

fifteen year old Jewish girl was able to write, "In spite of everything I still believe that people are really good at heart." These
words indicate her response not to the oppression that she experienced in her protective seclusion, nor to the puzzle of the grad-
ual disappearance of members of the Jewish community, nor to
the dismantling of human trust in her neighborhood, but to an
interior dynamic inviting her to hope in spite of her material
surroundings.

Again, a Christian believer might have identified that
dynamic as the Presence, inviting the young Anne to respond to
its offer of hope within the tensions of the Jewish community of
1943–1945.

Robert Bolt authored the 1960 play "A Man for All Seasons"—a third historical documenting of the traces of the Presence. In the play Bolt developed the person of Thomas More as
one who "could not be accused of any incapacity for life, who
indeed seized life in great variety and almost greedy quantities,
who nevertheless found something in himself without which life
was valueless and when that was denied him was able to grasp his
death."[16]

However, Robert Bolt himself identified his religious faith as
neither that of a Catholic, nor in any meaningful sense of the
word that of a Christian.[17] Yet, he had discovered in his personal
response to the character of Thomas More an option which motivated him to revise his meaning of human life.

For example, in the play the imprisoned More is visited by
his wife Alice and his daughter Margaret. In a plea to her father
to return to the life of convenience which was his if he recognized
Henry VIII as head of the Church of England, Margaret asked,
"But in reason! Haven't you done as much as God can reasonably
want?" To that Bolt had More respond, "Well . . . finally . . . it
isn't a matter of reason; finally it's a matter of love."[18]

That response was fashioned by Bolt, the non-believer. He
had found within his non-believing spirit a dynamic that proposed
a revision of the significance of life. To live had become a value
not because of a reasoned argument, but because of More's
response of love to the present God in whom Bolt does not
believe.

Again, a believer could have identified that dynamic within
Bolt's spirit as the Presence who offered an invitation to respond
to a new manner of evaluating human choices.

These traces suggest that the Presence is actively influencing
human consciousness. The human responses to the Presence here

identified are all revisions of values and choices. The opting for these new choices revises the values which secular conventions endorse. Nevertheless, somehow within the silence of their consciousness these persons opted to respond to a silent dynamic's invitation to revise human values. Their options were so altogether novel that the persons who chose them had decided to act in manners that revised the patterns of behavior in which common sense conventionally acts.

Persons who have chosen so to respond by revising human values can appear to be out of step with conventional values. They can appear to have lost their sense of how to respond to life in a proportionate manner. Nevertheless, they appear to be aware of the traces of the Presence. Moreover, they appear to be acting in harmony with physicists who envision the universe as pulsating or who imagine that the shortest distance between two points is a geodesic.

These latter persons also appear to be out of step with conventional values; their understandings diverge from the common-sense images of the world.

Common sense can assume that the universe is static, that straight lines are the shortest distances, that there is nothing within the world apart from that which can be verified by sense experience. There may, indeed, be no three-dimensional images that contemporary physics can use to clarify its revisions. Nor may Camus, Franck, or Bolt be able to direct persons to sense data that explains their responses to the subtle dynamics of their consciousness. However, physics has discovered non-three-dimensional evidences suggesting the pulsations of the universe, the geodesics between points, and curved space as the framework of the universe. Physics has not repressed these evidences simply because there have not yet appeared three-dimensional images of the meaning of the universe that can be expressed in non-mathematical concepts. Similarly, the sensitive persons cited have responded to the subtle dynamic operating within their spirits, though they would not be able to convince common sense that this dynamic is actual.

There are evidences within the world of human consciousness that there is a Presence who is actively influencing persons to choose values that are revisions of conventional values. There are evidences that indicate a subtle dynamic active within human spirits.

Not only is the Presence beyond the range of human sensibility, the Presence is also beyond human comprehension. Yet, to be open and vulnerable to the Presence is possible, even though one cannot intellectually comprehend its purposes in influencing human experience.

This chapter has been reflecting upon such implications of general relativity physics for the meaning of and response to human consciousness.

There is a convergent value in reflecting upon Einstein's method of discovering these revisionist descriptions of general relativity.

He had begun by questioning the assumption that every rational postulate of physics had to be deduced from experience. The absolute postulates of the physical universe were, perhaps, derived rather from the intellectual level that transcends concrete experience. Therefore, while he attended to experience, he was always careful to observe the intellect's awareness of the aberrations in experimental data from the patterns assumed to be normative.

When he attended to such aberrations, he allowed his intuitions to play freely with the experience and to leap from it to abstract postulates.

For example, he acknowledged the need to vary the frames of reference in measuring different times and distances. From that verified method he leapt to the intellectual postulate that time and distance can be calculated accurately from any reference frame. This diverged from the assumption that there must be a universally applicable frame of reference. "There must be a free invention of the human mind," mused Einstein, in order for humans to discover the postulates that might advance the comprehension of the physical universe.[19] He was certainly not urging science to deny the immediate experience of the world; on the contrary, he insisted that science begin there. However, he assumed that the interpretation of the experience of the world is derived not from experience, but from conceptual imaginings. The tools of comprehension cannot be found in the sensual order. Therefore, Einstein insisted that he, as well as every physicist, must allow the imagination to play freely with the experiences that relate the person to the physical world.[20]

This method enabled Einstein to articulate the aim of science that he had pursued. His aim had been, first, conceptually to comprehend and adequately connect sense experiences in their full diversity, and second, to accomplish this aim by the use of a minimum of primary concepts and relations. Only with this method could he attain the greatest possible logical order and a unity of the world picture, i.e., the logical simplicity which he sought. Only thus could he hope to attain his aim of comprehending experience. His aim, interestingly, was to comprehend, not to verify experience.

Yet, he would not accept comprehension without experiment, nor experiment without adequate description.[21] While experimenting may discover new data, e.g., the reddening of stellar nebulae, the data is in need of an adequate description developed by the free play of imagination joined with conceptual rigor, before the mind can combine the new data with new conceptual ideas.

As a result of his use of this method, Einstein was able to fashion the new view of the physical universe. So novel was this that it revised the assumptions of classical physics. It was so revisionist a view of the physical universe that it flatly contradicts common sense notions of the physical world.[22]

Therefore, only those persons have valued Einstein's revision of the meaning for the universe who have been willing to surrender their common-sense prejudices about what the physical world must be and to reformulate the assumptions about the foundations of all physical meanings.

Albert Einstein himself would later become reserved in his surrender to imagination's conceptions about the world. As will be seen in the following chapter, contemporary physics' revision that there are random occurrences in elementary matter led quantum physics away from the determinism of classical physics and to a non-determinist view of matter. Yet, Einstein was to insist until he died that physical occurrences had not yet been demonstrated to be random; he remained committed to the deterministic vision of meaning. The vision of the material world that was grounded upon random spontaneity required an openness that the later Einstein himself was slow to demonstrate. However, this will be discussed later.

The aim of this essay remains the exploration of the harmony between the attitudes of contemporary physics toward the world and the proclamation that the kingdom of God is at hand. This kerygma of the kingdom proposed an imaginative attitude toward the meaning of the world of human consciousness. It proposed that the Presence in the world offers new choices and new values to all persons.

However, just as accepting the new world-view of relativity is possible only for those persons willing to accept a new world-view, so accepting the kerygma of the kingdom is possible only for those who are willing to surrender common-sense prejudices of what the world of human consciousness must be. If there are persons who, like the later Einstein, are unwilling to surrender those of their assumptions about human consciousness which conflict with the kerygma of the kingdom, then these will find that they need to withdraw from the community that recognizes the validity of the Presence. Such persons will be forced to isolate themselves from the community of those more open-minded persons who accept, along with the new world-view of physics, that world-view proposed by the New Testament.

Persons who have selected this essay for their reading have learned to venture into novel intellectual pursuits. A venturesome mind is a blessing; a person who is an adventurer by nature can perhaps maintain his venturesome approach to life. However, it is difficult to fashion and to maintain such a disposition toward meaning. Yet, some persons can become adventurers by learning. These persons have discovered that in any venture they may encounter new options and new possibilities for the significance of their experiences. They need to avoid the temptation to narrow their focus so as to perceive only those options which they anticipate. If they so narrow their vision, they will certainly not venture upon new ground, but only upon an expected program. A venturer needs to keep the mind so free from habitual patterns of thought that one is ready to accept even that which is revisionist in what one encounters. This person is able quickly to put aside assumptions, to doubt the obvious explanation of that which he meets, and to entertain the possible value of any interpretation of his experience that presents itself. The person who has such a state of mind, moreover, needs to maintain confidence in self. Otherwise, the continual challenges which one encounters in venturing might appear to be vacant. Then the person will tend to direct the mind to ready-made interpretations, rather than to those that one's imaginative leaps might intuit.

Albert Einstein had been able to maintain the mind of the venturer when in 1905 he proposed that light energy was a particle phenomenon, though he knew well that light energy had been proven to be a wave phenomenon. He had been able to remain free of that habitual pattern of thinking of classical physics and to allow his mind to play with the evidence. He had been sufficiently self-assured to question the established explanation of light energy. He had entertained new, previously unimagined possibilities of explanation, even though these opposed the classical explanations.

He then was a model for the kind of openness that is asked of the person to whom the Presence in the midst of the human community is proclaimed.[23]

The person who has opted to read this book is a venturer and has some degree of respect for the revisionist interpretations of contemporary physics. Otherwise, this book would not have been opened. Hence, the reader has already learned to be suspicious of an absolute claim for the evidence of sense experience. He or she has learned that the sense experience which perceives the continuity of matter does not perceive matter as it is understood by physics. This person accepts the interpretation of matter as composed of innumerable discrete atoms; this one also acknowledges the need for physics to revise the common-sense perceptions of Newtonian space and of Newtonian time with the space–time of general relativity. This person recognizes that the vision of the universe that is derived from common sense is very different from the vision of the universe as fashioned by contemporary physics.

The same reserve about the criteria of sense experience as a norm of judgment is a value in considering the domain of human consciousness. There is a common-sense perception of human consciousness, a common-sense evaluation of the dynamics of consciousness, and a common-sense judgment of the source of these dynamics. However, the person who has selected this book has learned the value of turning aside from common-sense judgments and of allowing the imagination to play freely in considering the events within human consciousness.

The imagination of Einstein played enough to intuit that the universe is pulsating. This was an intuitive consequence of an imaginative reflection upon apparently inconsequential evidence: gases in galaxies fall below a certain critical level of density. This has appeared to observers as a color shift of the galaxies to a red.

Albert Einstein leapt imaginatively to interpret this color shift to be the increment of the acceleration of the red galaxies in motion away from the milky way galaxy. He concluded that the universe as a whole is now in process of expanding. Clearly, this astonishing conclusion is quite a distant leap away from the evidence, i.e., quite distant from the observation of red gases. Nonetheless, the free play of imagination upon the data had allowed

Einstein to intuit that the fundamental meaning of the universe
needed to be revised.

This was the method which Einstein urged that science must
use in any scientific search for meaning. The aim of science is not
to discover empirical evidence, but to fashion imaginative explanations of the empirical evidence that it addresses.

Similarly, the evidence that there are extraordinary dynamics
within human consciousness can be expected to require a leap at
least as great as was required in considering the evidence of the
reddening of the galaxies.

This essay has been undertaken precisely in order to reflect
upon some of this extraordinary evidence of consciousness which
suggests the dynamic of the Presence within human consciousness. The chosen paradigm for the revision of human meanings
based upon such evidence is the revision of physical meaning rep-
resented by the relativity of distance and duration and the interpretation of gravity as geometry. These infer that enigmatic data
within the physical world might be comprehended only by revising the assumed meaning for such data. Imaginative reflection
upon human consciousness suggests, moreover, that there are
other conventional assumptions that need to be revised. The
assumption that the life forms upon the globe are made up only
from organic, biological life may need to be modified; there could
be a living Presence that is neither organic nor biological. Enigmas within biological life, e.g., the unique appearance of artistic
genius in a genetic line, suggest that, perhaps, there is an influence within biological life that is not itself part of that life. There
are hints of evidence, however tenuous, that have been taken to
infer the Presence as active in human consciousness: for example,
some acutely sensitive persons have imaginatively envisioned the
Presence or the kingdom of God as active in the midst of human
consciousness. They have fashioned this kingdom, however, in
images very different from the images that common sense might
expect of the presence of God.

Among such sensitive persons' experiences are those cited
self-transcending experiences of Albert Camus, Anne Frank, and
Robert Bolt. Others are the cited experiences of those persons
who attend to and respond to the self-transcending dynamics of
their interior spirits. Such persons are aware of a dynamic that
acts within experience, though this interior summons cannot be
sensed and can easily be ignored.

Such hints indicate that there is operating within human consciousness a Presence that motivates some persons to act in extraordinary manners. Reflective persons have intuited from these hints that the Presence is active in human consciousness. As was the case in the discovery of the physics of relativity, only a free play of imagination can envision that the Presence is actively influencing human consciousness. The hints are only suggestions, not hard evidence.

The search for evidence of the Presence in this essay imitates the method of Einstein, not that of the positivists. Positivism would restrict its methodology to sense experience and common sense. Positivism allows only that meaning which is determined by the apparent stability of the senses. It concludes, therefore, that assertions or convictions which cannot be verified by empirical sense experience have no meaning.

Imagination, however, provides access to and comprehension of enigmatic data such as the extraordinary patterns of human behavior that are hints of the Presence.

This essay's reflection upon the world-view of contemporary physics as a harmonious counterpoint to the proclamation of the kingdom of God recognizes the need to attend to such hints within experience of extraordinary events within human consciousness. Furthermore, it is ready to fashion meaning from those hints, though such meaning may be quite far removed from that which conventional wisdom might assume the signs of the Presence would be.

However, if this leap to the imagination is not taken, then the logic of thinking on a grand scale will be no more possible in pondering the kingdom of God than it was in pondering the general relativity of the physical universe. So, in reflecting upon human consciousness, the fertility of imaginative insight needs to be allowed to make its contribution in the search for a path that leads to an understanding of the content of consciousness. The logic of common sense, i.e., a logic limited to the domain of sense experience, must not be allowed to determine the meaning of all influences within human consciousness.

Rather, reflection needs to imitate physics' leap away from the logic of common sense and sense experience. This leap was possible in the discipline of contemporary physics partially because of the development of the extraordinary telescopes constructed in the twentieth century. These confronted observers with data that could not be grasped in common-sense terms. Moreover, particle accelerators that probe the fundamental structure of matter have required physicists to seek for imaginative interpretations of the newly discovered physical data that common sense could not explain, much less imagine. The following chapter will consider specifically the domain of matter which these accelerators have been discovering.

Imaginative methodologies are required to discover in this new physical data the meaning of the subtle dimensions within the universe. Thus, it appears that imagination is required to discover meaning in the extraordinary dynamics of human consciousness.

However, before such methodologies can be applied to the dynamics of human consciousness, the person reflecting must be open to the discovering of revisions of the meaning of the world.

Many persons will not be able to reflect with such an openness. To many persons the products of imagination and leaps away from sense data appear to be idealistic fantasies. However, the method of proceeding used and defended by Albert Einstein in his monumental papers on relativity theory in 1905 and 1916 was just such a use of imagination. He then defended such imaginative play, such leaps, to be scientific hypotheses, not fantasies. With his liberated imagination, he was able to fashion a new integration of time, motion, and gravity. The result has been a new and fruitful vision of the physical universe. The result has been, as well, the new physics and its consequent technological discoveries that have transformed the twentieth century's culture in the west.

The young Einstein, the paradigm for those who reflect upon the meaning of the dynamics of human consciousness, was free enough of conventional manners of thinking to experiment with radically new postulates about the physical world.

This chapter on new world, Albert Einstein, and relativity has been focusing upon Einstein's model of openness to revisions of meaning and to the consequences of his choices in his physics of general relativity. This model exemplifies the intellectual attitudes appropriate for reflection, as well, upon the world of human consciousness. Moreover, Einstein's imaginative refashioning of the fundamental significance of the physical world is also an example of the insecurity that was required in the dismissal of the classical vision of the universe that had been adequate for almost three hundred years. He had to be willing to give up the security that is available in stable, widely accepted knowledge.

The purpose here, however, has been to direct attention to

the dispositions required in the study of the world of human consciousness.

Next the essay turns to new options of meaning available in quantum physics. The purpose of this new object of focus is, however, the same, i.e., to demonstrate that the vision of that physical universe, even within the very small dimensions of subatomic particles, implies that there are, within the familiarity of the world, occurrences and dynamics that can easily by overlooked or ignored. However, those persons who are open to revisions of the meanings of the world, i.e., to imaginative revisions of former meanings of that world, and to the vulnerability that results from such openness may be able to formulate or to recognize revisions of the fundamental meaning of human consciousness.

The positivists' demand that all meaning be verified in sense experience has been abandoned by contemporary physics. In spite of that, the positivists' criteria for meaning continues to attract westerners, probably because of its clarity and power.

Nevertheless, those who take seriously the kerygma that the kingdom of God is in the midst of humanity must imitate contemporary physicists by confronting the positivists' denial of the revisionist meanings of the kingdom because of the proclamation's failure to satisfy the criterion of positivist meaning: sense experience. Believers, therefore, need to be ready to abandon both their own common-sense assumptions which support the positivist criterion and the positivists' vision of the meaning of human consciousness.

The essay now turns to Max Planck and to his quantum physics in yet another effort to demonstrate that those who have discovered new options for the meaning of the physical world have done so only because they have been open to revisions of their prior comprehensions of the occurrences within the world. These persons have been willing to use imagination to revise the fundamental significance of the world. They have chosen to become vulnerable to the consequences of their new and imaginative vision and have accepted their own radical revisions of meaning. The intellectual attitudes manifest in the men who developed the physics of quantum mechanics can serve as models alongside the model of Einstein for those who reflect upon the world of human consciousness.

3

....

New World: Quantum Physics

Special and general relativity physics are two specialties within physics that have discovered that there are presences within the world that elude the range of that which the senses can grasp. However, quantum physics as well has creatively uncovered the traces of such presences. These quantum occurrences continue the challenge to the common-sense assumption that unaided sense experience is alone able to discover those events which occur within the world. These occurrences also reveal, as had the measurements of relativity physics, that the demanding methods of physical science have concluded that there are within the world presences that suggest that the Presence of the kingdom is at least plausible for Christian believers who are sympathetic to physical science. The Presence of the kingdom is not more extraordinary than the remarkable and explosive presences of relativity and quantum physics.

Quantum physics discovered its new presences within the world as a consequence, initially, of addressing unexplained problems within classical physics. It then proposed imaginative resolutions for those problems; these appeared at first to be implausible, yet later to be plausible enough to command wide respect. Quantum physics has thus been able to discover the unexpected presences within the world because it had moved unto uncharted lands, where it riskingly ventured into that vulnerability that results from imagining non-sensuous occurrences. It had surrendered the security that physics had found in the stable knowledge of classical physics. The venturesome physicists who risked a revision of the classical Newtonian physics were not protected by the confidence inspired by a verified body of knowledge. However, their vulnerability had allowed them to discover a perspective upon the world which opened onto unexpected events and even presences within the world. Therefore, the physical occurrences that are located at the subatomic level and at velocities close to the speed of light came into the focus permitted by the imaginative perspective fashioned by quantum physics.

This is a probe into the harmony between the kerygma that the kingdom of God is at hand and quantum physics. Those who seek for the traces of the kingdom might profitably attend to the openness and vulnerability of quantum physics as paradigms for the manner of proceeding in uncovering traces of the Presence within the physical world.

The present chapter, therefore, continues the discussion initiated in the reflection upon special and general relativity. The purpose now will be to consider the verified hypotheses of Max Planck and of those who followed his lead. The chapter addresses the intellectual methodology that allowed Planck to fashion his new world vision, i.e., allowed him to imagine unsensed presences within the physical world.

Max Planck was born in Germany in 1858; his doctoral studies were at the University of Munich. In 1900 he made his significant contribution to the founding of contemporary physics. He proposed a revisionist interpretation of the radiation of heat from a solid material object.

The physical problem which Planck had been studying is known as black-body radiation. This is the manifestation of increments of heat-energy in various colors of light from a body of metal that is being gradually heated. When the body of metal is cool, it emits a color that is located near the black end of the color spectrum. It, thus, is described as a black-body. However, when that body is increasingly heated, eventually the metal changes suddenly from the color black to red, without taking on the intermittent stages of color. If the heating of the body then continues, eventually the color of the body again suddenly shifts from red to white. Again, no intermittent tones of color between red and white are emitted.

Classical, Newtonian physics had hypothesized that the colors emitted by such a heated body should gradually have changed in a continuous emission of light of each of the colors between black and red and, then, between red and white. All the intermittent colors should have been emitted, not the leaps in color that were observed. The emission of discontinuous colors, thus, had been a significant problem for the physics of Isaac Newton. Nonetheless, Newton's hypotheses had continued to enjoy their privileged position of being the foundation for the physics that had been used by all western scientists for the three hundred years between Newton's career and Planck's research.

Max Planck's proposal in 1900 was that the discontinuity in the emission of colors in the experiment known as black-body radiation was a result of the atomicity of action. Atoms or quantum packets of energy within the body that was being heated were, he proposed, being stimulated. The body can, therefore, emit not continuous waves of light, but atoms, i.e., discrete packets of energy in the form of light. The discrete quanta, i.e., the packets of light of the black color, were emitted until the heat of the body reached a certain critical level. Then, quanta or packets of red light were emitted until the increasing heat of the body reached a second critical level. Then, atoms or packets of white light were emitted. These packets of light were identified by the new hypothesis to be discontinuous from one another. Planck's explanation for the discontinuous packets of light was that the various energy packets of discrete hues escaped from discrete kinds of atoms. This revisionist proposal described black-body radiation by appealing to the atomic composition of matter.

This quantum theory of the emission of atomized packets of energy went on to explain that electrons and other atomic particles of matter in metal obeyed not the laws of classical mechanics, but the revisionist laws of quantum physics. According to these laws subatomic particles are always in motion in independent, discrete orbits about the core of atoms; particles in one discrete orbit are emitted in forms peculiar to that orbit. Thus, when there is a change in the conditions of the atoms, e.g., when heat is increased in atoms, the energized particles change from one orbit to another and thus take on the incremental, energized behavior that is peculiar to the new orbit.

This revisionist quantum theory of matter went on further to recognize that particles were somehow associated with the waves that specifically identified discrete levels of heat in the containing body.[1]

These are physical presences within the world that completely elude detection either by the senses or by common sense.

Nonetheless, the revisionist interpretation by Max Planck had ignored these waves in its envisioning all matter as particles that are "granular" or discontinuous. This explained why the black-body, or any metal body, emits (or absorbs) energy only in discrete atoms or packets of discrete particles. Furthermore, it explains that because the particles are from different orbits, they are thus of different hues or colors.

These packets came to be identified as quantum packets or quanta of energy.[2]

Planck had revised the classical view of matter by insisting that matter and the physical universe in general were to be interpreted as fields of energy in various orbital systems. All physical matter is, Planck insisted, a collection of "grains" of energy that are discontinuous and discrete.[3]

Planck had opened the door. The meaning of the physical universe was not to be the same thereafter.

Then, in 1905 Albert Einstein made another of his momentous contributions to the revision of the meaning of matter by demonstrating that light, as well as matter, was quanticized. He demonstrated that in the photo-electric effect light consisted of particles or photons. Although James Clerk Maxwell, the Scottish physicist, had demonstrated in the nineteenth century that light is an electromagnetic wave, Einstein revised this in demonstrating that light can also be observed to be a beam of particles. Not only had Einstein modified the interpretation of light energy, he had also revised a verified hypothesis concerning the meaning of light and had pushed forward the frontier of quantum physics by demonstrating that light energy is, as Planck had hypothesized, made up of quanta of energy.

However, unable to dismiss the verification that light was a wave, Einstein proposed that there must be a wave-particle duality in light. He attempted in vain to reinterpret this duality so as to resolve the apparently contradictory characteristics of light.[4]

That duality has not yet been reconciled. A startling presence in the occurrences of energy and light had been discovered.

Seven years later, Niels Bohr pushed Planck's new meaning of quantum energy further. Born in Denmark in 1885 and holding a doctoral degree from the University of Copenhagen, Bohr dispensed with another hypothesis of classical physics by applying the quantum theory of Planck and Einstein to the domain of atomic structures. He proposed that, because energy is discretely quanticized, the electrons in orbit about the nucleus of an atom can exist only in certain, discrete, specific orbits. They cannot exist in any, random, orbital relationship with the nucleus. These electrons are able to jump from one specific orbit to another; however, they cannot jump into an orbit that is not already established.[5]

Thirteen years later, in 1925, Arthur H. Compton and A. W. Simon reconfirmed the remarkable presence that Einstein in 1905 had discovered in the photoelectric effect by demonstrating that the emission of individual photons of light obeys the laws of the conservation of energy. They scattered individual photons in a Wilson cloud chamber. They then observed the tracks of these individual electrons. Their observation succeeded in demonstrating that light, interpreted as particles, had been conserved in being scattered. Light exists as particles. This again questioned whether the classical electrodynamic hypothesis that light is present only as a wave was the univocal presence of light. In the Wilson cloud chamber the tracks of individual electrons were observed to behave in a manner suggesting that light is made up of individual electrons.

Niels Bohr concluded from this experiment that the time had come to acknowledge "a profound revolution in the concepts on which the description of nature had until now been founded."[6]

In order to demonstrate to the physicists of western culture that this revolution had, indeed, occurred, Bohr selected a number of young, bright physicists from Europe, the United States, and the Soviet Union to study the problems of the atom in what became the Niels Bohr Institute. Bohr convinced these young intellectuals that they were contributing to a scientific revolution which would transform the understanding of the material universe. They dedicated themselves to discover presences within the world by revising the meaning of elementary material occurrences. They were able to do this, however, only to the extent that they could put aside the convention of classical meanings that they had learned. They then were creatively open to new meanings, new presences, and even to the risk of insecurity in probing for revisions of the meaning of matter.

One of these free, creative, open, and risking young physicists was Werner Heisenberg, born in Germany in 1901. He proposed the creative revision of the meaning of the atom that rejected the value of fashioning an image of the atom, but proposed that the meaning of the atom was to be identified only from its function or from its effects.

In 1925, Werner Heisenberg completed his paper on this new mechanics. His new proposal was that the atom is not comprehensible in terms of electrons circulating about the nucleus, as in a miniature solar system which many physicists were then using to interpret the atom, but in terms of how the atom interrelates with other atoms. The atom functions as the source of energy transitions.

Therefore, energy transitions are the identity of atoms. Atoms are presences within the world that cannot be described, but only asserted as operating within the world.

There is manifest in such an understanding of atoms an analogy between atoms and the Presence. Just as atoms are non-empirical presences within the world, so too the Presence is believed to be non-empirically within the world.

The analogy can be expanded as the understanding of the atom developed. Heisenberg described the atomic interactions in various arrays of numbers which follow observable rules that were calculated by using mathematics' matrix theory.[7]

This is the Heisenberg equation, an unprecedented step in the revision of those occurrences present in the foundations of matter. To comprehend matter now is to recognize the functions that it performs, not to fashion an image of what it is.

Simultaneously, even as the creative work on the meaning of the atom was being harvested by Heisenberg in Denmark, Louis de Broglie in France was proposing yet another revision in the manner of thinking about the atom.

De Broglie had been born in 1875 into an ancient French family of diplomats, politicians, and soldiers. However, he had chosen to study physics. He earned his doctoral degree at Marseilles University.

The revision which De Broglie initiated was to verify Einstein's duality of light as a wave particle. He confirmed this duality by diffracting electrons of light energy around a material obstacle. The electron particles, upon hitting the obstacle, behaved just as waves would be expected to behave: light behaved both as particles and as waves.

Erwin Schroedinger had similarly confirmed this duality in 1926. Born in 1887 and educated at the University of Vienna, Schroedinger devised an equation that the electron would have to satisfy if it was, indeed, a wave in a hydrogen atom. The electron satisfied the equation.

This equation has been considered to be the beginning of what has been identified as "wave mechanics."

Then in the same year, in June of 1926, Max Born modified the de Broglie–Schroedinger interpretations. They had specified the probabilities of finding an electron at various points in space. Born proposed that the electron was always to be considered a particle. However, the location of the particle remains only a probability. The value that Born found in the de Broglie–Schroedinger "wave" equation is that it identifies the probabilities of locating the electron particle at various points in space.

Born, whose birth in Germany was in 1882 and whose education was at Goettingen University, had revised the interpretation that de Broglie had introduced. In place of interpreting light as a duality, he insisted that light is not to be considered as a wave, but always as particles. There is not a duality of presences in light energy; light is present only as particles.

Particles' location upon particular axes, however, can be discussed in terms of waves of probability. Furthermore, according to Born, even though the presences understood as location, momentum and energy of particles may not be able to be imaged, they are still to be considered always as particles. The inability of physics to envision those characteristics of particles had allowed particles to appear as though they were waves. However, these are only waves of the probability of locating the particles. They are not, according to Born, magnetic waves.[8]

Born eventually modified his initial revision of the meaning of the de Broglie–Schroedinger wave equation. Although he had first argued that the de Broglie–Schroedinger wave equation had been able to identify the probable location of an electron, he eventually put aside that interpretation.

In its place he attempted to resolve the wave particle duality by arguing that the de Broglie–Schroedinger wave equation specifies the probability that a particle will have a specific energy level corresponding with a single point on the axis of the frame of reference.

The issue, however, is that Born, too, had departed far from classical, Newtonian physics in this acknowledgment of a probability within the physical world.

Classical physics had insisted that every energy level for any particle of matter and, thus, for any atom at any point on a frame of reference is determined.

Born, however, argued that the research of de Broglie, of Schroedinger, and of the new quantum physics in general led physics to the need to deny that the energy level of a particle could be identified as determined specifically at any location or moment. There had been a time, Born conceded, when physicists had been confident enough that their knowledge of the physical world had enabled them to identify the determined levels of energy at any point in a coordinate frame of reference.

However, that time had passed. As a result of the theory of the quanticization of energy and as a result of the consequences of the apparent duality of light, all had changed. Indeterminism had been discovered to be a characteristic of the foundations of matter in the world.

Therefore, the measurement of determined, specific levels of energy had to give way to probable estimates. The discovery of the waves, which Born identified as waves of probability of the energy levels of particles at various locations, was evidence that some physical occurrences are fundamentally not determined, but are probabilities.

As a result, the experiments of physics have been forced to put aside the search for determined and absolute knowledge of the energy level of particles. There is no determinism in particles' radiating as energy nor in their decaying into alternate energy levels. Instead, physics must be content with knowing the world as indeterminate at the micro-level; there knowledge is restricted to calculations of the probability of occurrences.[9]

This brilliant interpretation by Born of the implication of the de Broglie–Schroedinger wave equation was a giant, influential step toward the radical revision of the deterministic world-view of classical physics. Previously, the physical world had been understood to operate with the determinism of a well-built clock. However, after Born's interpretation, the non-determined world-view of quantum physics became a legitimate point of reference: the occurrences of the world operate not with the precision of a great clock, but with the contingency of a pinball machine.

Gradually, more and more physicists are accepting this world-view: the new physics is able to make only statistical predictions. The determinism of classical physics does not fit the world-view suitable for the subatomic level. Fewer and fewer physicists are accepting the deterministic world-view that claimed the power to predict precisely all physical occurrences. Determinism at the microlevel had been discovered to be non-existent.

This revision of the image of the foundations of the physical world confirms the implication of the physics that has been thus far considered; namely, physical science has evolved to discover that it cannot identify exhaustively all of the physical occurrences within the world. On the contrary, science has become increasingly aware that there is present within the physical world a multitude of physical occurrences which can be grasped only symbolically.

There is critical significance of this evolution in scientific knowledge in the face of the present search for traces of the Presence. Just as science has come to acknowledge that the physical occurrences, i.e., the physical presences within the world, cannot be known with the precision of determinism, so this study acknowledges this probability of physical occurrences as a directive to undetermined but faint traces of the Presence within the world.

There has been a general acceptance of the importance of what came to be known as Niels Bohr's principle of complementarity and Werner Heisenberg's uncertainty principle. These two efforts to distill meaning from the indeterminacy of the physical world became the Copenhagen interpretation of quantum theory. This interpretation, formulated at the Niels Bohr Institute in Copenhagen, rejected determinism and objectivity as characteristics of the matter at the microlevel of subatomic particles. In place of these it asserted the uncertainty and complementarity of the physical events within the world.

The uncertainty principle asserts that the one who measures the identity of a particle cannot settle on both the precise position and the precise momentum of a particle. Physics can, however, calculate the uncertainty of the identification of a particle's position in relation to its momentum. Similarly, physics can calculate the uncertainty of the particle's momentum in relation to its position. This uncertainty principle has demonstrated that there is an indeterminacy, rather than a determinism, at the foundations of matter.

The principle of complementarity asserts that every occurrence on the subatomic level maintains an established relationship between the particles and waves within the occurrence. Particles and waves, therefore, are complementary concepts. Moreover, to measure one of these properties, e.g., the wave of an electron, is to alter the identity of the other property, e.g., the identity of the particle. Physics can no longer claim objectivity in its measurement of the physical world. On the contrary, physics eliminates objectivity precisely in its measuring of the world.

This principle of complementarity deserves to be explained. The study of one property of an electron, e.g., its momentum, is possible only if some measure of energy is added to the electron in observing it. That energy is an increment to the prior energy of the electron; thus, as a result of observing the momentum of the electron, there is an addition to the energy of the electron. As a result of that addition of energy, the momentum of the electron is increased. Thus, the objective identity of the electron is necessarily changed in studying it.

This absence of objectivity in observing the subatomic world must occur because there is as yet no method of observing the occurrences in that world without adding energy to that world.[10]

Nonetheless, there is an objectivity in quantum physics; yet, it is the objectively statistical probability of occurrences within the subatomic world, not objectively certain occurrences, not objectively determined occurrences. This objective probability at the quantum level is derived from Heisenberg's and Bohr's equations, which reinterpret the electron's apparent dualism as wave and particle.

Nevertheless, the Copenhagen interpretation of quantum physics had proposed that the calculation of a statistically probable occurrence within the micro-world is the only significant measurement available to quantum physics.

Moreover, there is another significant consequence of the Copenhagen interpretation. Physics must specify the experimental arrangement by which elementary particles are observed and measured in order to identify the altering effects of the observation upon particles. These experimental methods differ in their altering of the energy level of particles. For example, the experiment that illuminates particles with the addition of the energy of a beam of light alters particles differently from an experiment that adds increments of energy to accelerate particles. Because any experiment upon elementary particles alters the particles in some manner, elementary particles have come to be recognized as, in part, an observer-created object of study.

Thus, the objective determinism of particles had been dismissed from quantum physics as no longer a scientific description of matter. In its place, determinism-by-the-observer had been acknowledged as the significant influence upon any elementary particles that are observed.[11]

The identity of the presence of occurrences within the physical world at its most fundamental level had, thus, been significantly revised. The prior identity of an occurrence firmly established, i.e., objectively determined events, had been disestablished.

Furthermore, the presence of a startling, newly discovered occurrence had been disclosed: observation itself alters the energy level of elementary particles; observation thus abolishes the prior conviction that occurrences are physically determined;

observation discovers that all subatomic occurrences are probable, not determined.

After quantum physics had evolved for thirty-one years, Max
Planck, who had begun the study of the micro-world and had initiated the revisionist world-view of quantum physics, formalized
that new world-view in his 1931 book, *The Universe in the Light of
Modern Physics*. He there articulated the presence of the previously unknown dimension of the physical world that had resulted
from the discovery of the presence of the occurrences observed
by quantum physics.

This formal recognition that there exists a previously
unknown dimension of the world-view of elementary matter was
needed not only because many physicists had been suspicious
about a dimension of the world in which determinism does not
exist, but also because Max Planck had formally asserted that
there is within the world a physical dimension that had been
totally unknown to humanity prior to the twentieth century.
Planck, however, needed to demonstrate that it is plausible to
defend the presence of a physical dimension that can be grasped
neither by the senses nor by common sense.

> In physics, however, as in every other science, com-
> mon sense alone is not supreme; there must also be a
> place for reason. Further, the mere absence of logical
> contradiction does not necessarily imply that everything
> is reasonable. Now reason tells us that if we turn our
> back upon a so-called object and cease to attend to it,
> the object still continues to exist. . . . Such is not nec-
> essarily the case.
>
> It is considerations of this kind, and not any kind of
> logical argument, that compel us to assume the exis-
> tence of another world of reality behind the world of the
> senses: a world which has existence independent of man,
> and which can only be perceived indirectly through the
> medium of the world of the senses, and by means of cer-
> tain symbols which allow us to apprehend apart from
> the senses.[12]

Contemporary physics had discovered the existence of a
world that is accessible to humans only by symbols.

Those symbols, however, are so sophisticated that very few
persons have the necessary training that permits this access. Most

persons can live their lives as though there were no such world. Nevertheless, quantum physics has discovered that behind the world of common sense, behind the world of the senses, and even behind the world of logical consistency, there is present a world that had always existed, but that has only come to human awareness in the twentieth century.

Unfortunately, however, apart from those few members of the human community who have studied quantum physics, persons find the micro-world too esoteric to be taken seriously.

Significantly, however, the increment to the understanding of the universe which quantum physics has identified has had remarkable consequences upon the known world. This micro-world has changed the world-view of that which makes up the macro-world. One such consequence has been the shattering of the familiar world-view envisioned by positivistic philosophy. That world-view's criterion of meaning (only those assertions have meaning which can be verified in sense experience) has been dismissed in the micro-world. The vision of the world that has appeared because of the new perspective of contemporary physics is that there are occurrences within the world that lie far beyond the range of sense experience.

Max Planck had endorsed this new world-view: "The structure of this physical world consistently moved farther and farther away from the world of sense and lost its former anthropomorphic character. Still further, physical sensations have been progressively eliminated, as for example in physical optics, in which the human eye no longer plays any part at all. Thus the physical world has become progressively more and more abstract; purely formal mathematical operations play a growing part, while qualitative differences tend to be explained more and more by means of quantitative differences."[13]

This assessment of the symbolic, abstracted character of the physical world deserves to be respected. Any persons who choose to dismiss as irrelevant the symbolic, abstract world-view of quantum physics are choosing to dismiss a foundation for the technology which has transformed the culture of the west in the twentieth century.

Thus far, quantum physics has been considered to be the study of the presence of occurrences within a new world that appeared either in the experimental work of the laboratory or in the symbolic reflections upon the significance of that research.

The chapter now shifts its focus to the implications of this new world-view for various communities. It begins with the community of physicists. However, this shift is undertaken with some caution; the next several pages will move even farther from the consideration of the kingdom of God, which is the center of this essay. Yet, these considerations will reveal, as the proclamation of the kingdom of God asserted, that the new perspectives with which to observe the presences within the physical world suggest new perspectives from which to perceive the Presence in the world.

Max Planck had discovered that quantum packets of energy were emitted from a heated black-body of metal. Those quantum packets were discontinuous, i.e., separated from one another by a definite measurement that has come to be known as Planck's constant. The significance of this is that the quantum packets are made up of quantities that are integral multiples of a definite constant, h. Another manner of expressing this discontinuity is to argue that the foundation of matter is a quantified separateness. All matter is separated by multiples of h among elementary particles. This h, Planck's constant, is identified as 6.626 ($\times$) 10^{-32} joule. A joule is the unit of work or a measure of the work done in moving an electrical charge one unit of distance toward the direction of force. This can also be expressed by identifying a joule as approximately 50% greater than an electron volt. It is, indeed, an extremely small unit of work.[14]

Clearly, Planck's constant is a most small unit of measure. It is so small that for the experience of common sense it is totally insignificant. However, in the micro-world of contemporary physics, it is most significant in identifying the discrimination between discontinuous packets of energy. It therefore cannot be dismissed.

This evidence of the importance of Planck's constant is its repeated appearance in the equations and inequalities of contemporary physics.

Werner Heisenberg found, for example, that the constant was essential in order to express the degree of irresolution in his uncertainty principle of 1927. Heisenberg's principle, a mathematical inequality, approximates the measurements of the momentum and position of an electron. The inequality can be expressed:

$$\Delta p \times \Delta q \geq h,$$

i.e., the error in the position, Δp, times the error in the momentum, Δq, is always greater than h.

The explanation of this inequality is that the product of the measure of uncertainty of an electron's position and the measure of the uncertainty of the electron's momentum, if these are made simultaneously, is never less than h, where h is Planck's constant.

Another manner of expressing this is to say that the nearest that instruments can approximate the precise measurement of both the position and the momentum of an electron is not less than an error of h. Thus, Planck's constant is also significant in discriminating the limitation within which physics must operate in measuring properties of electrons.[15]

The implication of Planck's constant for the present study is that there operates within the physical world an unidentified force (or field) that maintains a separation between all packets of energy. Nevertheless, physics cannot identify this force other than to measure it. Thus, this is yet another physical presence within the world that cannot be grasped either by the senses or by common sense.

Another example of the importance of Planck's constant is the measurement of the quanta of electrons escaping from the surface of a substance. Electrons leap from metal surfaces when the metal surface receives sufficient increments of energy. Electrons are thus effectively boiled from a surface when particles from an external heated source strike the surface. The kinetic energy of these incoming particles can transfer to the particles already on the surface an amount of energy greater than the amount of energy that binds the electrons to the surface. These electrons, then, have sufficient energy both to satisfy the attractive force of the surface that binds them and to move away from the surface.

They can also leave the surface if they are extracted from the metal by a strong external electric field.

By whatever process the electrons escape from the surface, they leap away in the form of quanticized packets named photoelectrons.

The significance of Planck's constant in this research is that each photoelectron has a level of energy E identified thus: E = nhv, i.e., the product of n, h and v, where n is an integer, h is Planck's constant, and v is the frequency of the wavelength of the incoming electrons.

Planck's constant thus again identifies the discrimination between discontinuous matter. It represents the presence of an actual force within the physical world that has been measured in calculating the discontinuity in packets of energy and the level of energy of escaping photons.[16]

A third example of the importance of Planck's constant is in the identification of the levels of energy that can be emitted by atoms.

Atoms function as oscillators. An oscillator is a mechanism that fluctuates between various actions or positions. In the case of atoms there is a fluctuation between various frequencies of energy being emitted.

However, atoms do not have and apparently cannot have just any level of energy; they can have only those levels which are values of E in the above equantion, $E = nhv$. Thus, the level of energy that is radiated by the atom is always a quantity equal to integral multiples of h in $E = nhv$. The atom, in radiating energy, oscillates between radiating a unit of energy that is one integral multiple of h of energy and radiating another unit of energy that is a different integral multiple of h. This can be interpreted to mean that energy is radiated in quanticized or discrete packets, but not in a continuum of energy, i.e., not in measures of energy between integral measures.[17]

Planck's constant is, thus, a mathematical quantity identifying the discreteness of the oscillations of energy radiated from atoms.

The validity of this perspective has been verified by numerous experiments.

In 1913 James Franck and Gustav Hertz verified the quanticized packets of energy by passing randomly energized electrons through a gas of sodium and then, immediately, through a gas of hydrogen. If the initial energy of the electrons had been less than a certain minimum, i.e., less than one level of nhv in the above equation, then the electrons passing through the gases would have emerged with the same velocity with which they had entered, i.e., they could not have increased the amount of energy that they possessed. On the other hand, if the initial energy had been greater than the certain minimum, but not great enough to equal the next integral level of nhv, then the electrons would have lost that excess energy as they passed through the gases.

The electrons all emerged from the gas with specific, integrally discrete levels of energy, even if they had initially been charged with what had appeared to be levels of energy that were not integral multiples of *h*.

The Franck–Hertz experiment had demonstrated that every atom has only packets of energy. Moreover, it demonstrated that every atom can accept only integral multiples of these packets. If less than integral multiples of energy are offered to the atoms, the atoms prune away the excess energy in order to trim the energy to a size that it can accept as an integral packet.

The experiment, thus, had demonstrated the validity of Planck's constant as a discriminant of the discrete packets of energy in all matter.[18]

As physics continues to discover smaller and smaller elements of matter, Planck's constant continually emerges as the discriminant of each element.

Before considering the implications of quantum physics for the material world at large, the chapter pauses here in order to consider the significance for physics of Max Planck's discovery of the previously unknown presences within the world of matter.

The classical laws of physics had been discovered and verified by Isaac Newton in the late seventeenth and early eighteenth centuries. Newton's laws had brought order to the visible world of objects and temporal events. These laws had discovered the determinism and the objectivity that would come to be identified with all objects and events in the visible world. For almost three hundred years these laws of classical physics had provided a completely adequate perspective from which to address the problems of the physical world.

Then, at the very beginning of the twentieth century quantum physics broke away from the classical world-view of Isaac Newton in virtue of its new hypotheses for the occurrences at the level of the subatomic phenomena. Quantum theory turned away as well from common sense. At the micro-level of the material universe quantum experiments demonstrated that occurrences are not determined, not objective, but random and subjective. Thus, at that level, Newtonian determinism and objectivity appear to be simply irrelevant.

Those who choose to be aware of the world of quantum physics have learned that there are occurrences present within the world that the human senses cannot grasp. They look at the physical world from a new perspective. They have learned to think no longer in deterministic and objectivistic terms. Rather, they have come to expect to discover only probabilities in subatomic phenomena. They have learned that even a modest involvement with the phenomena of the micro-world changes those phenomena, that even a modification in the manner of being involved will further modify the phenomena that are observed. Consequently, they have learned to consider occurrences at the subatomic level as, always and necessarily, a reflection of the effort to observe them, i.e., the phenomena are observer-created.

Furthermore, the physical world that is observed at the subatomic level is a multi-dimensional world. Humans can be considered to live in a four-dimensional world, i.e., the three dimensions of depth space plus the dimension of time. However, the micro-world manifests many more than the four dimensions in which human life is embedded. As a result, those who observe phenomena in the micro-world are observing occurrences that unfold in more dimensions than the human mind can comprehend or imagine. Nevertheless, scientists attempt to measure these phenomena and to express these measurements in the language of the four-dimensional world of human experiencing. Their expression of that which they had observed is, therefore, at their own admission, quite different from that which they had observed. The problem in expressing subatomic occurrences is that there is no human language, not even a highly symbolized language, that has been developed to express adequately the multi-dimensional micro-world of subatomic particles and their interactions.[19]

In so complex a world, the human mind has been thus unable to make predictions of the future. Future-oriented deterministic prediction may be possible in the macro-world of objects and temporal motions of position and velocity. There the human mind has been able to grasp the causes and effects of occurrences so that it can predict the future events that are being determined by prior occurrences. However, in the micro-world this has proven to be an impossibility. Such determinism and such idealistic comprehension are pure fantasies in the subatomic world of elementary particles and their interactions.

Thus, there is a need to fashion a world-view which uses criteria different from the determinism and objectivity that were standards within classical physics. The quantum physicist studies a unique physical world. He needs to acknowledge this uniqueness as a limitation under which he studies.

Such was acknowledged by Werner Heisenberg.[20] His fundamental principle concerning the subatomic world denies the possibility of comprehensive knowledge of the whole of any situation in the micro-world. It denies that quantum physics is able to predict determined occurrences in the future. Nevertheless, it acknowledges that the quantum physicist is able to calculate the mathematical probabilities of certain future occurrences. However, it insists that there is no presence that is certain and determined at the micro-level. In place of the objectivity that Newtonian physics would have assumed that particles must have, it insists that the occurrences present among particles manifest only a mathematical "tendency to happen."[21] This principle clearly and unambiguously insists that there are in the micro-world strict limitations upon those who study this world.

Quantum physics envisions that there are present within this physical universe occurrences that interrelate differently from the manner of occurrences of macro-objects that are studied by classical, Newtonian physics. Moreover, this specialized discipline of physics has fashioned a method of representing those occurrences and of measuring the interrelations between them. Thus, the fact that these presences are completely veiled from human perception has not prohibited contemporary physics from carefully discussing the influence of the presences upon one another and upon the macro-world.

Subatomic particles can be observed to behave in a manner that suggests that they have made decisions based upon decisions made by other particles. Sets of electrons can be identified as correlatives of one another because of that correspondence of interrelating by correlative decisions. When one subset of these electrons develops in a certain manner, then another distinct, distant subset of electrons can be observed to develop in a corresponding manner. This latter subset appears to have developed as a result of its decision to evolve in response to the development of the prior subset.

The word "decision" is used here because the second subset is apparently responding to an occurrence within the prior subset, though there is to human perception no apparent communication between the two subsets separated by a significant distance.

The two subsets can be quite far removed from one another. They can be separated by the length of a room or even by several miles. Apparently the interaction would occur regardless of the distance between them. In every researched case, regardless of

the distance between the subsets, the second subset still responds
to the occurrences of the prior subset by an apparent decision
that is based upon the developments within the prior subset. In
the world of elementary particles there appears to be an intercommunication and a sensitive responsiveness that appear to persons in the macro-world to be decision-making.[22]

Another argument for the existence in the micro-world of an
inexplicable intercommunication and interrelating is the occurrence which is known as tunneling. This will be discussed at
greater length later in this chapter. However, at this point it is
briefly cited to indicate that there are present within the world of
subatomic particles occurrences which appear to be impossible in
the world of common sense.

Tunneling describes the escape of elementary particles confined within an area with barriers thought to be impenetrable.
The particles can exit from the area in which they are confined
and can then appear in an area from which they had been isolated. Quantum physics does not have an explanation for this tunneling. Little can be asserted about this occurrence other than to
acknowledge the probabilities that predict whether or not tunneling might occur, where it might occur, and over what distance
the particles might relocate. Obviously there is present there an
occurrence which common sense finds inexplicable.

A third argument for the unobservable presences within the
world of subatomic particles is that identical particles in that
world will respond to different spatial contours by suddenly manifesting unexpected variations in behavior. For example, particles
in one geometrical dimension of space interrelate differently
from their identical particles in a different geometrical dimension. This variation of movement appears to be determined by the
geometry of the spatial region. The geometrical variations of spatial contours, however, are so very small that the untrained
observer would be unable to notice them. The regions about
which we are speaking are the regions inside of an atom or a mol-
ecule. Nonetheless, a variety in the geometrical dimensions of different atoms leads to a variety in the behavior of the particles
within them.[23]

It is a further confirmation of these unobserved presences to
attend again to yet another reconfirmation of Planck's constant
as a discriminant of quantum occurrences at the micro-level: the
frequency of every wave of an electron is a multiple of Planck's
constant, h.

Further, the correlation between movement of every wave and the area confining particles correlative with the wave was verified by Erwin Schroedinger in 1926.[24]

These observables in the micro-world lack the kind of objectivity, the kind of determinacy, and the kind of certitude that have come to be expected of the observables in the macro-world.[25]

Nevertheless, these characteristics combine with the micro-world's non-objectivity, randomness, and observer-created characteristics to lead quantum theory to conclude that the elementary physical world is essentially non-substantial presences.

The elementary physical foundation of the physical universe is made up not of substances, but of fields: there is nothing more.[26] A field is a homogeneous medium which has in all directions, without boundaries, the same physical properties with the same values, measured along axes in all directions. The significance of asserting that the fundamental bases of matter in the universe are fields is that the phenomena of matter in the physical universe result from the interactions of unobservable, non-substantial presences which propagate through large, undefined areas. The physical world, thus, is made up fundamentally of non-substantial presences.

Thus, to assert that the non-empirically based Presence of the kingdom operates within the physical world is not more radical than to identify the foundations of the world as basically fields.

Clearly, this interpretation of the meaning of the physical bases of the universe is radical. Radical reinterpretations demand radical changes in language. Yet, because human language is taken from ordinary life, the language of quantum physics appears less than radical. It is much closer to human life than is the discovery of fields as the bases of all matter.[27]

Before considering those specific discoveries about the physical universe that have resulted from quantum theory's field-reinterpretation of the fundamental elements of that world, the reader might benefit from a series of reflections upon the quantum theory that introduce quantum theory's reinterpretation of the foundation of the matter of the world in which we live.

The study of the foundations of matter in the universe has discovered the micro-world of matter, which had been assumed to be an ordinary presence, to be a unique presence. It has even established the credibility of the non-sensory presences and of their ultra-rational dynamics that operate upon familiar physical objects. The characteristics, therefore, of sensibility, rational consistency, and determined location are not to be considered to be the absolute descriptions of the world, as these are treated in the macro-world.

The world of human consciousness and presence might similarly include the presence of occurrences that are non-sensory, ultra-rational, and beyond predictive comprehension.

Among these non-sensory dynamics which might operate in human consciousness, the Presence can thus be considered to be plausible, not a fantasy, even if it is non-sensory, ultra-rational, and beyond comprehension.

This is a consequence of the discovery by the study of the micro-world which suggests that, whenever persons turn their attention away from the familiar macro-world to the more elusive dimensions of the world, they have to put aside the familiar logical consistency that applies to ordinary experience. Quantum physics has discovered a dimension of the world in which there are presences which are not ordinary. The dimension of the world in which the Presence operates should be expected to be no less extraordinary. Just as the presences within the subatomic world require a revision of the meaning in the world of ordinary experience, so, too, the Presence in the world of human consciousness can be interpreted, but as requiring general revision of meanings in the ordinary world.

Moreover, the general revision of meanings derived from the micro-world suggests that the human consciousness which structured this revision is at least as awesome as the revisions which it fashioned. The intricacies of the universe are mirrored by the intricacies of the human creation of mathematics that describes physics. Thus, the complexity and volume of data found within the human consciousness that created mathematics might be assumed to be at least as awesome as the complexity and volume of data in the physical universe. Just as the data of the physical universe does not appear to be reducible to a system of comprehension, so too the data of human consciousness may not appear to be so reducible. The data of consciousness, perhaps more complex and more voluminous than that of the physical universe, might require an even more powerful system of comprehension than mathematics if the dynamics of the world of consciousness, such as the Presence, are to come into focus.

In the search for such a system, persons can discern some of the subtle data of human consciousness that need mutual interrelating.

The revision of meanings within a consciousness is required because that consciousness confronts unsensed physical presences, unknown physical presences, and the Presence. This appears to be one of the principal subtle characteristics of consciousness that needs to be fundamentally restructured in relation to the world.

In the world of the occurrences of physics this revision has been the cardinal pivot for understanding. Revision of meaning for physics was required in the turn from classical physics' comprehension of objects as continua of matter to the comprehension of discontinuous, random, discrete atomic structures as the fundamentals of matter. In a similar manner, contemporary physics had to revise its assumption of the solidity of matter to a comprehension of physical foundations as being located in ever smaller elementary particles.

This listing of revisions in physics could continue; however, the need to revise meanings as a result of new presences must be evident as a demand made by the fundamental structure of the physical world.

The revision of meaning can be expected to be demanded by the dimension of human consciousness, as well.

However, the yet to be revised common-sense understanding of human consciousness has been consciousness has been based upon understandings drawn from ordinary experiences. Nevertheless, common sense has been shown to be generally inadequate in comprehending the foundations of the physical universe. Consequently, common sense is less likely to be adequate to comprehend the domain of human consciousness, where a more elusive dynamic is present. Thus, those fixed conventions and assumptions about human consciousness that are anchored in common sense are to be considered as only tentative.

This study proposes that there is a parallel structure between quantum physics' interpretations of the physical world and the interpretations of human consciousness. Ordinary human consciousness can be discussed in terms that are drawn from ordinary experience. However, there are experiences of a Presence within human consciousness that are as far removed from ordinary human experiences as occurrences of the micro-world are removed from the motions of the macro-world. Thus, just as there was a need for quantum physics, so there is a need for an appropriate method of interpreting the extraordinary events of the Presence within consciousness. This interpretation will have to be a radical revision of the method of interpreting ordinary experiences.

Karl Rahner's reinterpretation of human consciousness acknowledges an extraordinary dynamic or Presence operating in human experience. Because of this transcendent dynamic some experiences have been so far removed from the ordinary human experiences that they require a revision of their meanings, values, and choices. Clearly, then, such transcendental human choices have needed to be located in a frame of reference as extraordinary as the Presence or dynamic that influences those choices.

Albert Camus, Anne Frank, and Robert Bolt have already been presented as examples of experiences of persons who have responded to this transcendental dynamic present within their consciousness. There are, of course, many other persons who similarly respond to experience in a manner that suggests that there is a dynamic operating within their consciousness that is not reducible to a quantity. The presence of this dynamic challenges other persons to recognize the presence within consciousness that revises the common-sense interpretations of the meaning of human choices. There are persons who choose not for the purpose of gaining rewards or avoiding punishments. These choose because of some sort of a non-conventional presence within consciousness.

This study recognizes the need for a heuristic with which to interpret such a dynamic. The Presence as the motive in such choosing has appeared to some persons to be an appropriate heuristic or system for interpretation. The symbol of the Presence appears in the reference frames of persons who place such trust and confidence in those movements within their consciousess that they behave according to the manner that they believe that movement or the Presence suggests to them. Extraordinary persons such as Joan of Arc, Mother Teresa of Calcutta, and Jean Vanier of l'Arche come to mind. The decisions of their lives can be understood only by those who admit that these persons have relationships with a non-empirical Presence within their lives. However, there are also quite ordinary persons whose lives suggest that the dynamic of the Presence operates within their consciousness. For example, there are persons, some of the little people, who offer themselves while the wider public takes no note of their self-offering.

The heuristic with which to comprehend such behaviors might be an analogue of the heuristic of quantum physics. That heuristic has put aside the criteria of determinism and objectivity in judgments within the subatomic realm.

The Presence appears similarly to operate non-determinedly and non-objectively within human consciousness.

However, such an oblique Presence would be ignored or denied by those persons who so earnestly seek to be secure that they refuse to acknowledge extraordinary experiences within their consciousness. They choose to suppress any personal experiences which arise only from a movement within consciousness. Other persons, however, less concerned with the security of personal convenience, might acknowledge the extraordinary movements within their conscious experience and choose values which appear to convention to be foolish.

The discussion concerning the wave-particle duality, which this chapter will soon resume, had identified the later Albert Einstein as having become more reserved about surrendering his own security derived from the physics of classical determinism. He withdrew from the community of quantum physicists because of their hypotheses concerning the micro-world. Einstein judged that the revision demanded of classical physics by quantum physics was premature. He was confident that further research would confirm the established heuristic of Isaac Newton's seventeenth century, classical view of the world's determinism. He insisted that as complex as the world might be, it was not as non-determined as it had been described by quantum physics. So, he isolated himself from those in the world's scientific community who, in his opinion, too readily were accepting the drastic, revisionist world-view of quantum physics.

This danger of isolating oneself from the human search for understanding and of refusing to acknowledge a transcendental context lies before those persons whose initial response to the possibility of the Presence operating within consciousness is that it is either fiction or fantasy. These persons prefer their own heuristic of consciousness as superior to the revisionist heuristic which, similar to the heuristic of quantum physics, acknowledges a presence within consciousness that cannot be reduced to empirical causes.

The chapter now shifts its focus from its consideration of quantum physics world-view's implications of non-empirical presences within the world to an integration of these novel meanings for the world. These presences have been discovered in the dualism of light–energy, the probabilism of the occurrences within the microworld, and the complementarity manifested by particles in the universe. These presences lead reflective persons to an awareness of how extraordinary the physical world is: there are far more dynamics active within the world than human sense perception is capable of perceiving.

The stimulus that had led to the discovery of these dynamic, non-sensuous presences was the the hypothesis of wave–particle duality by Louis de Broglie in 1924.

A brief history of the research upon which de Broglie depended will clarify the significance of his research.

In 1803 Thomas Young had provided the first argument for physical dualism. He had experimented with light rays from the sun. He had experimented with the event of solar rays by studying how solar light passes through two screens to a detector wall. In the first screen there was a single slit or hole. The rays from the sun passed through this slit and then struck the second screen. In the second screen there were two slits; both of these or only one of these could be covered with a piece of dense material that could block the ray of light. The rays of light needed to penetrate this second screen in order to reach the detector wall. Thomas Young was interested in observing how the rays were detected on that wall in two distinct situations: first when only one of the slits in the second screen was opened, then when both of the slits were opened.

When only one of the slits in the second screen was opened, the rays of light were detected in a distinct, clearly defined focus or circle of light.

When both of the slits were opened, then the detector wall registered alternating bands of light and darkness. These bands can be visualized as successive ellipses alternately light and dark. Of these bands or ellipses, the center band was the brightest; the bands on either side of the center band were bands of darkness; the bands outside of those two bands were light bands, though this light was less intense than the light in the center band. Bands outside of these were bands of darkness. This alternating pattern continued.

This alternating pattern of bands as observed on the detector wall when both slits were opened is a phenomenon of wave mechanics that is known as interference. Interference results from the diffraction of waves; diffracting waves of light overlap and reinforce one another—bands of brightness. Diffracting waves also cancel one another—bands of darkness. This pattern of interference in Thomas Young's 1803 experiment with sunlight led to his interpretation that light is wave-like.

For one hundred years, i.e., for the entire nineteenth century, physicists had concurred: light was wave-like.

Then, in 1905, Albert Einstein contributed the second argument. He had demonstrated that light is particle-like. Physics had long recognized the weaknesses in Young's argument. One of these was the unanswered question of how the rays of light that entered the first screen were informed about the number of open slits in the second screen. The rays of light passing through the first screen appeared to manifest different forms because of the number of open slits in the second screen. When one slit was open, the light manifested itself in a particle-like manner; when both slits were open, the rays of light manifested a form that was wave-like. However, physicists had been puzzled by the apparent communication to the incoming light concerning the number of open slits in the second screen.

Prompted by this enigma, Einstein experimented not with that apparent communication, but with the composition of light–energy. He hypothesized and then demonstrated that in the photoelectric effect, i.e., in the escape of light from a metal surface, light is not wave-like, but particle-like. He thus had demonstrated that light is a beam of photons or light particles.

As a result of Thomas Young's 1803 demonstration that light is wave-like and Albert Einstein's 1905 demonstration that light is particle-like, physics was confronted with a dualism in the composition of light–energy. This dualism seemed to describe a physical condition which in the macro-world is impossible. A single physical event, light–energy, was both wave-like and particle-like.[28]

In an effort to demonstrate this apparent impossibility as acceptable, Louis de Broglie researched the compatibility of waves and particles in a critical 1924 experiment. He developed a mathematical equation, lambda $= h/mv$, which equated the wave-length associated with matter, lambda, with the quotient of Planck's constant, h, and the product of the mass and the velocity of the particles under consideration, mv. Thus, the particles moving at a high velocity would have very small wave-lengths. These, therefore, appear to be not wave-like, but particle-like.

On the other hand, particles moving at a much decreased velocity would appear to be waves.

Consequently, in the world of ordinary experience, where momentum and velocity are generally decreased, the dualism of waves and particles does not appear. However, in the micro-world where increased velocities do occur, the dualism is manifest: light–energy manifests compatibility with waves and with particles.

As was noted earlier, Erwin Schroedinger concluded from this evidence that the compatible dualism that de Broglie had demonstrated in rays of light is a compatible dualism in electrons generally, not only in light–energy. As a result of this demonstration, subatomic particles have since been interpreted both as particles and as waves.[29]

Erwin Schroedinger then raised a new question: he asked what was waving in the phenomenon observed in the electron. This question followed from his having doubted that a particle could be simultaneously a wave. His education had not prepared him to accept dualism as a precise scientific analysis about an individual object in the world. Rather, he had been trained to approach an individual electron as either one identity or another, i.e., as either a particle or a wave, but not as both.

However, in the micro-world the interpretation of electrons as dualistic in behavior had appeared to be precisely appropriate. Analysis had been unable to deny that apparent dualism. Human research had been unable generally to predict which of the two behaviors, i.e., that of a wave or that of a particle, electrons would manifest in alternative experiments. When an experiment introduced energy to the electron, e.g., a beam of light to permit observation of the electron, this energy caused the electron sometimes to behave as a wave, sometimes as a particle. Therefore, physics had been unable to resolve the question about how to predict which form of behavior electrons would manifest. Consequently, physics had been unable to resolve this problematic dualism at the foundations of the physical universe.[30]

Whether the electron behaves as a particle or as a wave is determined apparently by the experimental situation in which the electron is observed. Thus, physics had been unable to analyze the behavior of an electron without including in the analysis the experimental situation in which the electron is observed.[31]

However, as noted earlier, in 1926 Max Born argued that there is no need to analyze electrons as both particles and waves. His intuition of the data of his research was that particles remain always particles, though in certain situations, e.g., when Thomas Young opened both slits in the second screen, particles are distributed in a probability scattering. Then the human observer discovers the particles to behave not as particles, but in a manner that manifests their mass, velocity, and probable locations.[32] Thus, that which is observed in Thomas Young's two open slit experiment is not precisely the particle's behavior as a wave, but rather the particle's exposure to a particular method of observation.[33]

In such an analysis, a legitimate interpretation of the observed photon or light–electron is that light is continuously oscillating electromagnetic fields. This analysis envisions fields (boundary-less regions having common physical characteristics) in oscillation to effect illumination or light, i.e., the oscillating fields result in illumination.

For example, a field oscillating light to transparent matter, e.g., a windowpane, is partially reflected and partially transmitted. However, the same field oscillating light to opaque matter, e.g., coal, is absorbed. In being absorbed by coal or by an opaque matter, the absorbed field then is identified as the energy heat. In this case of illumination light is identifiable as a beam of electrons. Illuminated coal manifests the photoelectric effect, i.e., the light that emerges from the matter is observed to be particle-like and is measurable in quanta or packets of energy.[34] This is a legitimate analysis.

However, this hypothetical intuition is not to be considered to be a verification of light as particles. The analysis is hypothetical because its intuition that light is observable as particles has not as yet been verified to be universally applicable to all matter, even if it is verified in its application to opaque matter.

Nonetheless, the analysis of light as fields does allow light to be comprehended as electromagnetic oscillations of fields. This is an approach to light–energy that considers light as a model for all subatomic energy.

In that model, light and all subatomic energy can be analyzed as electromagnetic interactions. In such a model the micro-world is envisioned as a world beyond the horizon of what can be imagined by the human mind.

Niels Bohr had identified this gap between the objects within the spectrum of what humans can imagine and the objects of the micro-world as his principle of complementarity. There is a critical gap between the actual occurrences or presences within the micro-world and the human comprehension of those occurrences.

Thus, his principle explicitly acknowledges the unresolved tension or the duality that physics confronts in subatomic research. It insists that the wave behavior and the particle behavior of electromagnetic emissions complement one another. Researchers may therefore choose to interpret any energy either as particles or as waves. However, after that choice has been made and after the energy has been interpreted, then the researcher must acknowledge that the interpretation is only partially complete. The alternate interpretation would also have been possible and correct. Choosing one analysis does not preclude the validity of the other.[35]

Clearly quantum physics was acknowledging that there were presences within the world of elementary particles that are mysteries to the contemporary grasp of the human mind.

The question by Schroedinger about what was waving had led to this precision in the world-view of the micro-world. Moreover, the analysis of the complementarity or the alternate interpretations of the micro-world illustrates the wonderous presences within that world. However, the analysis of that world has remained elusive for all, except for those physicists who are willing to admit in their analyses that presences implied by data may be other than that which common sense might expect and may lead to further ambiguous presences within the world.

The duality of the wave–particle behaviors of electrons has thus eroded that certainty about the presences within the world which western culture had expected to discover from its having endorsed Aristotle's "principle of non-contradiction," i.e., that opposing assertions cannot be made of the same individual object (or presence) at the same time. In the micro-world it is necessary to affirm the presences of two identities of the same individual object at the same time. Furthermore, the "either . . . or" mode of thinking that applies so often to the world in which humans live, where two presences of identities of the same object cannot be identified to be valid at the same time, is weakened as absolutely applicable to the world of human consciousness because of its inapplicability in the micro-world.

The chapter now shifts its focus again. After having reflected upon the revision of those presences required by the wave–particle dualism, it turns to yet another revision of presence implied by the recently discovered world of the quanta.

The vision of matter that has resulted from the seemingly endless discovery of ever more elementary particles is a discovery of presences as unexpected as that resulting from the dualism in elementary particles.

There had been unanswered questions concerning the composition of electrons and elementary particles. These had prompted physicists to investigate further into the properties of matter. There were questions concerning the basis for observer-created reality, questions concerning how particles can tunnel away from an area in which they had been confined, as there were questions concerning why electrons can appear in forms verified to be sometimes wave-like and other times particle-like, i.e., questions concerning the indeterminacy of electrons.

These questions left physics in a once-removed relationship with the occurrences which it considers. Physics had, therefore, constructed sophisticated, technical machines in order to observe occurrences in the micro-world and to find solutions to those questions. Because of this technology physicists can observe not the actual subatomic occurrences, but the manner in which their technological devices respond to the occurrences. These responses are then interpreted in an effort to comprehend more exactly the presence of interactions among the subatomic occurrences.[36]

As the responses of these instruments were more closely observed and more precisely interpreted, the community of physicists drew remarkable conclusions. One of these has previously been mentioned: the physical universe is basically a set of electromagnetic fields in which interactions of particles occur not in a manner that is determined, but in probabilities. These occurrences obey the principles of special relativity along with those of quantum physics. Thus, distances and temporal durations are relative (special relativity) to surrounding motions in the measurement of their interaction; in their interaction they exchange packets of energy (quantum physics). This latter conclusion led to the discovery of the interaction of packets of energy in terms of those interactions of the fields of energized quanta that were known.

This conclusion led physics to search for more fundamental interactions among fields and for the resulting quanta.[37] This search led to the discovery of the unsensed presences of ever more elementary forms of matter. Interacting within the fields of molecules, atoms, and nuclei, there are presences of forms of matter identified as hadrons and quarks, forms of matter that no human eyes have seen.

These new forms of matter were discovered when increments of energy were brought into interaction with energy already in the subatomic world. The resulting, instantaneously appearing and disappearing nuclear interactions were interpreted to signify the emergence of what have been judged to be the presence of ever new forms of matter.

These nuclear resonances, or mechanistic responses, first came to be noted in 1952, when the technology had been developed which was capable of supplying concentrated beams of protons to energy within the subatomic world. As a result of such increments of energy, the presences of hadrons and quarks were acknowledged.[38]

Hadrons were interpreted to be the forms identifiable by that which quantum physics interpreted to be interactions with the arbitrary term "spin." However, spin has been identified only in resonances that are registered in measurements that could be made with integers or half-integers. Those hadrons with the spin identified with an integer were named "mesons," while those with the spin identified with a half-integer were named "baryons."[39]

Hadrons, therefore, can be divided into three different presences or families or sets of quanta on the basis of spin: hadrons, mesons, and baryons.

The world of matter was clearly coming to contain far more presences than might have been assumed by those who consider only experiences studied by classical physics or who rely upon common sense and stop short of doing research at the quantum level.

There is present another form of matter more elementary than the hadron: the set of particles that are called "quarks."

The word "quark" is a German derivative found in James Joyce's *Finnegan's Wake*, where it refers to a curd of cheese. However, in quantum physics it refers to the presence of hadrons which have a spin identified with one half of an integer and which would be baryons, but which have only a fraction of the electrical charge that is found in baryons.

Of course, like the hadrons, the presence of quarks has never been seen. Further, like the hadrons, these can be distinguished only by certain mathematical responses in the mechanical detectors. These presenses are distinguishable by opposite electrical charges and by an appearance identified arbitrarily as an "up," a "down," or, finally, a "charm."

Quarks were discovered in 1968 at California's SLAC electron accelerator behind Stanford University. There a beam of electrons was fired at a proton target. The electrons scattered in concentrated point-like structures that were identified by symbols.[40] However, those presences instantaneously vanished. They had appeared only in the instant of the scattering of the electrons from the accelerator into the interacting fields of elementary particles in fields.[41]

Such appearances and vanishings appear as wonders both to physicists and non-physicists alike.

The wonders do not stop there.

Continuing the exploration into the foundations of matter, physics next bombarded even the quarks with increments of energy. As a result, where there had been a single quark, the presence of a new pair of elementary particles appeared—a quark and an anti-quark. The quarks, which had constituted the hadrons, had been multiplied, as earlier had occurred with the hadrons.[42]

Next, high energy accelerators again bombarded the quarks. As a result new sets of quantum presences named "leptons," "gluons," "muons," "neutrinos," and "taus" appeared.

These new presences, however, appear to be alternative forms of hadrons.[43] Thus, physicists have hypothesized that hadrons may be finally the ultimate material or the fundamental elements from which all physical presences in the universe emerge.

The hadron, or the ultimate material, displays an utter simplicity of structure. However complex the method of detecting the foundations of the world, the world of matter is far from being complex at its foundation. On the contrary, the physical world is ultimately a set of interacting fields. Penultimately, the fundamental presence of the physical universe is the delicate, simple, and elusive hadron.

The final consideration in this chapter on the unexpected, non-sensuous presences within the micro-world is a reflection upon the quantum reversals of that world. These reversals provide yet another perspective from which to observe the presences within the quantum dimension of the physical universe.

As has been repeatedly the case in quantum physics, the consideration of quantum reversals indicates that quantum physicists must be open to startling presences within the physical world.

The wave-particle duality and the seemingly endless investigation into the fundamentals of material elements require of physicists (and similarly of non-physicists) an openness to ever new presences emerging from the physical world. These new presences within the material world have required physicists repeatedly to revise their world-view derived from previous discoveries. If physicists had remained fixed in the understandings and the conceptual structure that they had learned from classical physics, for example, then they would have refused to acknowledge the new presences within the world that have been discovered in quantum physics. However, to the extent that they were able to remain open to newly discovered presences and to conceptual structures that were different from those that were classical, to that extent they were free to fashion a new world-view that envisioned the world to be made up from presences that had been completely hidden from all humans previously.

Moreover, the comprehensions of these presences are often the reverse of the comprehensions which both classical physics and common sense have accepted as self-evident.

Perhaps the most obvious crisis implied by these reversals of comprehensions is the crisis that follows from the reversal of Isaac Newton's classical vision of the determinism of the physical world. Newton had first discovered and then demonstrated the law that in the visible world of ordinary objects and motions, determinism reigns universally. Stones are determined to fall according to observable laws; planets are determined to orbit according to such laws; so, too, do rivers course; so tides ebb and flow. In all physical events there had been discovered a determinism and an objectivity.

However, this world-view is reversed in the microworld. Neither determinism nor objectivity is a criterion used to identify the occurrences there.

Not human perception, but technological machines observed the presence of the occurrences in the micro-world. Not sense-experience, but mechanical devices discovered the hadrons materializing or leaping into existence just there where there had been nothing. Non-human devices responded to the hadrons' subsequent vanishing or leaping out of existence. There is no known method of perceiving by the senses that these presences are determined to leap into and out of existence. Such are the extraordinary occurrences that have been acknowledged as the presences within the microworld.

However, such indeterminate and non-purposeful presences are altogether unknown in the world of visible objects and persons.[44]

There are persons who assume that the classical presences of the macro-world are mirrored in the presences of the subatomic world. That assumption needs to be reversed. Max Born's two-slit experiment demonstrates this need.

When the beam of electron particles is fired to the second screen with both slits opened, then the wall on the far side of the second screen detects the electrons in a pattern not of particles, but of the diffraction or interference that are characteristic of a wave. This wave-particle dualism reverses the classical interpretation that an individual presence, in this case the electron, is identical with itself in any variation. In the visible world an individual presence is always so identical with itself. It cannot be identified now as one individual and later as another. However, at the level of the micro-world this dualism of presences amidst electrons has been verified.

There is yet another reversal of meaning of the presences within the micro-world. Objects exist in various states at the same time. These various states can be observed if the physicist selects the appropriate method of experimentation.[45]

The assumed determinacy of the presences within the micro-world is further challenged by Schroedinger's cat-in-the-box experiment. This thought experiment imagines that a cat is sealed in a box along with a weak radioactive source and a detector of radioactive particles. The detector can be activated for only one minute. If, during that minute, the radioactive source emits a particle, the particle would be detected. The detector would then release a poison gas in the box. This gas would kill the cat.

Because the box is sealed, humans cannot know either whether the radioactive source did emit a particle at the precise moment or whether the poison has been released, i.e., whether the cat is alive or dead. Therefore, they cannot speak of the cat as being in a definite state. They could do so only if they were to break the seal and observe the actual state of the cat.

However, they can speak of the cat in terms of the probability wave that predicts its state. There is a meaning in speaking of the state of the cat as probably alive or probably dead.

The state of the cat is not determined in relation to human knowing.

Furthermore, this condition of probability is the description of the manner of existing of the electrons in Max Born's two-slit experiment. A mathematical probability statement is required to identify the electrons as waves or as particles. However, apart from a probability statement there is no accurate manner in which humans can speak about which path the electron used to pass through the second wall in the experiment. The electrons remain thus as an undetermined presence; they are not determined to be the kind of presence that passes through one slit or the other.[46] They, therefore, are not determined to exist either as waves or as particles, as the cat-in-the-box is not determined to exist in a determined state either as dead or as alive. In both the case of the electrons and that of the cat, the state of existence is not a determinism, but a probability.

Nevertheless, in the case of the cat-in-the-box the irreversibility of time has determined the state of the cat. Although human persons cannot speak accurately about the state of the cat except in terms of probabilities, the state of the cat has been determined by an event in time even before any human person knows the cat's actual state.

However, in the case of the electrons' path of passing through the second screen, not time, but the firing of the electrons appears to determine that path which the electrons take. There does not appear to be any information that is anywhere available about which paths the electrons must follow. On the contrary, there is every reason to doubt that there are determined paths for passage before the electrons are fired. This doubt is a consequence of the prior knowledge that electrons behave both as particles, which follow a single path through the screens, and as waves, which do follow a refraction and interference path through the screens.

In either case, physics must acknowledge the unpredictable locations of the electrons in the micro-world until the electrons have actually been fired. The power of physics to predict must therefore be laid to one side.

Although, in the world of ordinary experience, objects and persons exist in a predictable determinism, in the world of elementary particles occurrences exist only in unpredictable states of probabilism.

This reverses classical physics' assertion of the objectivity of all matter in the universe.

A final instance of the reversal of the identification of the presences of classical physics was demonstrated in the Einstein, Podalsky, and Rosen paper (EPR) of 1935. This paper demonstrated that quantum occurrences interrelate through action-at-a-distance. That violates the classical law of local causality. The paper demonstrated that according to the postulates of quantum physics causal occurrences at the quantum level have effects in locations that are far removed from the occurrences.

The EPR paper argued the action-at-a-distance of quantum physics in a thought experiment.

Two particles, 1 and 2, are located near to one another in New York at positions q_1 and q_2. The particles can be assumed to be moving with the respective velocities p_1 and p_2. Quantum physics is able to measure the sum, p, of such velocities: $p = p_1 + p_2$; so, too, the distance between the two particles, q, can be calculated, $q = q_1 - q_2$.

The thought experiment next assumes that the two particles interact in such a manner that particle 2 flies off to London, while particle 1 remains in New York. These two locations are so far apart that it is reasonable to suppose that what is done to particle 1 in New York should in no way influence particle 2 in London; that is the principle of local causality.

However, according to the laws of quantum physics the total momentum of interacting particles is conserved. Consequently, if someone measures the momentum of p_1, the particle in New York, then he can deduce exactly the momentum of the particle 2 in London: $p_2 = p - p_1$. Likewise, by measuring the position, q_1, of the particle in New York, one can deduce exactly the position of the particle in London: $q_2 = q - q_1$.

However, in measuring the position, q_1, of the New York particle, the person will disturb its momentum, p_1. This follows from the axiom that, in observing subatomic particles, some addition of energy must be added to the particle; that energy alters the momentum of the particle.

In altering the momentum of the particle in New York, one, thus, has changed the quantities in the equation above, $q_2 = q - q_1$. That is to say that the alteration in the momentum of the particle in New York has altered the momentum of the particle in London. There has, in this case, been action-at-a-distance.[47]

This reverses an axiom of classical physics: action-at-a-distance is inconceivable in the classical physics of Newton; nevertheless, in the micro-world of quantum occurrences, there are repeated violations of that law of local causality.

Meaning has been reversed; there are presences within the micro-world that are unthinkable within the world of sense experience.

Albert Einstein's analysis of this reversal of an axiom of classical physics was to reject the validity of the postulates that implied a world in which action-at-a-distance is possible; i.e., he rejected the validity of the postulates of quantum physics. He judged that the postulates of Newton's classical physics would continue to be valid, at least until quantum physics had done considerably more research. He judged as premature quantum physics' demand that physicists surrender the classical postulates.

The data of the new world of quantum physics had nonetheless been widely accepted. Many physicists were acknowledging that there are, indeed, occurrences within the micro-world that are impossible in the macro-world.

The theme of this essay is to present the kingdom of God as critical for human self-understanding. This presentation has proceeded by arguing that there are presences within the physical world that cannot be experienced by sense experience.

The essay has defended that these presences are actual occurrences. Thus, the first and second chapters turned to Albert Einstein and his physics of special and general relativity. These interpretations of the physical world revealed the novel presences that relativity physics has discovered within the world. These demand that a new frame of reference for the physical world be adopted.

In order to perceive the world from that reference frame persons must revise that comprehension of the presences within the physical universe that they have learned from common-sense experiences.

There have been persons who have been models of the openness and vulnerability needed for this revision of the meaning of the physical world. Albert Einstein was so open to the new presences in the reference frame of relativity that he put aside his previous world-view and his previous assumptions as less fertile for comprehension of the physical world than the world-view and postulates suggested by the new reference frame of relativity.

He represents an example of the positive actions that might

be imitated by persons to whom the kerygma of the kingdom and its Presence is preached.

Then the essay shifted in the third chapter to a consideration of quantum physics and the quantum world with its perspective upon the presences within the world. Quantum physics offers the reference frame which allows the presences at the foundations of the physical universe to be perceived as quite different from what common sense perceives to be present. This perspective of quantum physics is possible for persons with minds willing to revise their interpretations of the presences within the universe, persons who are willing to be intellectually vulnerable to the unknown consequences of assuming a perspective upon the world radically different from that which common sense assumes.

The quantum world is a dimension that is accessible neither by sense experience, nor by common-sense understandings, nor even by the classically verified world-view of the physics of Isaac Newton. It is a dimension that is accessible only through symbols interpreting mechanical responses of sophisticated technological devices.

Quantum physics has even introduced reversals of the meaning of the presences within the world. Yet, the physicist who was primarily responsible for developing relativity physics, Albert Einstein, judged that physics was not sufficiently prepared to accept such presences by rejecting the deterministic vision of the physical universe.

However, there have been other physicists, e.g., Max Planck and Werner Heisenberg, who chose to open themselves with little reservation to the quantum presences within the world.

They model a positive response to non-sensuous presences. Quantum physics had revised the meaning of matter as solid and continuous; they were open to this. Quantum physics had demonstrated that matter was discontinuous and composed of discrete packets of energy; they were open to this as well. Physics had gone on to argue that the interaction of elementary particles is random and occurs apparently without cause; even this was accepted. As quantum physics developed, its researchers hypothesized that there is a fundamental dualism in elementary particles: electrons are found to behave both in wave-like and in particle-like manners. The open-minded among physicists chose to accept even that startling revision of meaning.

Eventually quantum physics had introduced its fundamental perspective upon the presences within matter. Matter in the micro-world is the spontaneous interaction of fields; the presences there lack the determinism and the objectivity that classical physics had envisioned as necessary in all matter of the physical world. In order to interpret such interacting occurrences at the foundations of matter, quantum physics could use only probability statements. It could not use statements of certitude in such discussions. The open-minded and vulnerable persons who chose to accept this have been able to perceive the quantum presences within the world of matter. They have assumed a world-view that allows them to attend to presences that are unavailable to persons who have not so chosen.

Those physicists who have chosen to use the world-view of quantum physics are models and examples for persons who are considering the kerygma of the kingdom of God.

The kerygma of the kingdom announces the Presence as active among the human community; however, the Presence cannot be experienced by those who acknowledge only that which is perceived by the senses. Such persons are as closed as are those who acknowledge only the perspective of the classical physics. The gospels' proclamations announce that, because of the Presence that is active amidst the human community, believers need to adopt a perspective from which to perceive the unsensuous presences within the world. Thus, there is need for the change of life or the *metanoia* called for by the evangelists.

Those physicists who have accepted the revisionist world-view of quantum physics are paradigms of the openness and vulnerability which is adopted by those who accept the proclamation of the Presence.

4

....

The Presence:
The Kingdom of God Proclaimed

There is evidence of an enigmatic presence within the physical world. This Presence is suggested by the physical, yet imperceptible occurrences that contemporary physics has identified. Contemporary physics not only has recognized these occurrences, but has fashioned a system of quantitative thinking with which to reflect upon the interaction of these non-sensuous occurrences with physical elements of the world.

The initial three chapters have been an introduction to reflection upon that Presence. They situate the reader within an intellectual framework that enables the person to attend critically to the proclamation that God is present within human consciousness. The reader has discerned from those chapters that a person need not step aside from modern, educated western culture in order to envision the world as filled with the Presence of God. On the contrary, so to envision the world is analogous to the manner in which contemporary physics grasps unsensed occurrences within the physical world.

The presence of God in the midst of the human community is the New Testament's proclamation that the kingdom of God is "in your midst." However, such a proclamation can be considered to be a gratuitous assertion that persons can gratuitously accept or reject in the light of their personal dispositions. Therefore, the proclamation of the kingdom of God deserves to be investigated. Thus, the present chapter proposes to explore the accepted meaning that contemporary scholarship interprets the New Testament to present in its proclamation of the kingdom of God. This is the principal objective of the chapter.

Nonetheless, it also intends to investigate how persons might so focus human experiences so as to discover signs of the kingdom of God as present. It thus proposes a heuristic or a system to be used to investigate the meaning of the kingdom of God. Third, it proposes to identify those mental and psychological orientations that the New Testament proposes as appropriate so that persons might be able to perceive the traces of the kingdom.

Or perhaps a different focus might be more clear: it seeks what sensitivities the New Testament asks that persons should develop in order to relate to the presence of the kingdom. Such sensitivities cannot be overly subtle or mystical if persons are expected to respond naturally to the presence of the kingdom in their lives, i.e., if the kingdom is to be more than an object of devotion.

The first phase of the chapter will reflect upon the meaning of the kingdom as proclaimed by the authors of the New Testament. This meaning emerges from reflecting upon the kingdom as a symbol. Then the kingdom as proclaimed in the parables of the New Testament will be considered. Next the kingdom will be interpreted from the perspective of contemporary hermeneutics of the New Testament. Finally, the kingdom at the intersection of those three sets of data will appear.

The second phase will be a reflection upon a heuristic of the kingdom of God, i.e., a theological method of discovering the meaning of the kingdom.

The final phase will be a discussion of that which the heuristics discover the kingdom to be, i.e., a discussion of how to discover traces of the kingdom within human consciousness. Thus, the final phase will be an integration of the previous two.

The meaning of the kingdom of God has been obscured because it has been interpreted to be not a symbol but a concept referring to the church. This is considered to be a misinterpretation because the New Testament writers had presented the kingdom not as a concept but as a symbol.[1]

However, since the fifth century, the Christian tradition has interpreted the phrase, "the kingdom of God," as a concept. Augustine of Hippo had in the fifth century so interpreted the kingdom; moreover, Augustine had such influence that the Christian tradition followed his example. Christianity came to rely so confidently and unquestioningly upon the teachings of Augustine of Hippo that his teachings became models for Christian doctrine.

Furthermore, a consequence of Alaric the Hun's sacking of Rome in 410 C.E. was that the stability of Roman culture upon which Christianity had grown to rely was gone. The Roman church thus sought to discover some alternate foundation for its social stability. In place of the stable Roman culture as a foundation, an alternate base was sought to provide a durable security for the church. Augustine's writings were then positioned at that foundation in order to provide for western Christendom that stability which the Roman church desired in its expression of the meaning of faith.

Those writings exercised so great an influence upon the Christian tradition because of their position in the intellectual development of western culture. Augustine's intellectually refined writings had appeared to represent the principal, Christian heritage of Roman culture. This heritage was recognized in Augustine's blending of the rich heritage of Roman philosophy with the Christian thought of the fifth century. Consequently, Christianity could pridefully present its doctrines in their Augustinian format.

Augustine's works were evaluated as so focal a center for Christian culture that they exhaustively determined the mold in which western theology was to develop for eight centuries. Even Aquinas' thirteenth century shift to a theology derived from Aristotle did not displace Augustine from the center of Christian culture. Evidence of Augustine's continued importance is manifest in his sixteenth century influence upon Martin Luther and his seventeenth century influence upon the Jansenists.

Augustine's interest in speculating conceptually had been motivated by his intent to discover the meaning of ecclesial doctrine; he was little interested in the symbolic meanings of the New Testament. Consequently, the Christian tradition, imitating his model of doctrine by concept, interpreted the kingdom as a concept. Christianity had, consequently, detoured away from the symbolic intent of "the kingdom of God." It failed to exhort believers to allow that symbol to form their manner of acting and valuing. It presented the kingdom of God to believers as Augustine had in his *City of God*, i.e., as identified with the totality of redeemed humanity. The kingdom thus came to refer to the victory of the church in winning the totality of humanity as believers.[2]

Even the cosmic range of this interpretation, however, would eventually come to be narrowed. In the middle ages the kingdom of God was to become a concept that referred to no more than the hierarchical church in history.

This restricted meaning of the kingdom differed greatly from its symbolic meaning for the authors of the New Testament. In the earliest Christian community's songs of praise, in its exhortations to live in the presence of God, in its openness to experiences as encounters with God, and in its similes and parables of God's active presence in the human community, the earliest Christians had used the kingdom of God as a symbol to evoke the myth of "God-acting-as-king."[3]

Such appears to be its significance, moreover, in the New Testament.

However, western culture had evolved to become more philosophically oriented and less disposed to think symbolically. Thus, after the time of Augustine symbols no longer evoked myth. Thereafter, the symbolic language of the New Testament was quite facilely reinterpreted conceptually as indicating the relationship between the church and the salvation of humanity. Its original purpose of evoking the myth of God's activity as king had fallen first ito disuse, then into oblivion.

A change in this interpretation occurred in the late nineteenth century with Johannes Weiss (*Die Predict Jesu vom Reich Gottes*, 1892). Since then the recognition had been dawning that there is a relationship between myth and symbol in the New Testament's use of the phase "kingdom of God." Weiss' contribution to the discussion had been to direct attention away from the conceptual manner of interpreting the kingdom and toward its pristine use as a symbol in the New Testament authors' proclamation. He perceived that the New Testament had not presented the phrase as referring to the church. Weiss proposed that the kingdom had initially connoted an apocalyptic, divine "storm" which was to break out in order to destroy and to renew the world. Because of this apocalyptic event, Weiss interpreted the New Testament writers to have summoned persons to examine their ethical ideals and to change their hearts ("metanoia").[4]

Rudolf Bultmann then carried this reinterpretation further with his thesis on the New Testament's use of "the kingdom of God" (*Jesus*, 1926). He proposed that Jesus had used the term "kingdom of God" as a demand that humans were to decide about their relationship to the activity of God within their lives.

Nevertheless, both of these interpretations were conceptual; they remained within the Christian tradition's boundaries that limited the use of "the kingdom" to the domain of concepts. Weiss' concept was a change of hearts; Bultmann's, the critical choice to be made by each believer in deciding how to relate to God.

The discussion on the kingdom was then directed along quite a different path by C. H. Dodd (*Parables of the Kingdom,* 1935), who argued that those who are interested in comprehending the meaning of the kingdom of God need to study the parables of the New Testament. Such a proposition was based on his thesis that the parables proclaim the presence of the kingdom of God as having begun with the ministry of Jesus.

Thereafter, Christian theology has acknowledged the parables of the New Testament to be crucial in the discussion concerning the meaning of the kingdom.

This turn to the parables eventually had the effect of redirecting the attention of Christian theology to the kingdom of God as a symbol. This resulted from Dodd's perception that the proclamation of the kingdom was expressed not so much in the New Testament's theology as in its parables. Moreover, this turning to the parables also led eventually to the recognition of the wealth that symbols convey in indicating the dynamics of the symbol "the kingdom of God."

Many of the parables are introduced with the clause, "The kingdom of God is like. . . ." This introduction announces that the referent of the parables is the presence of the kingdom. More importantly all the parables refer explicitly to the common, ordinary experiences of the hearers of the parables. The images are imaginative reconstructions of familiar situations from the common milieu of first century eastern Mediterranean culture. Thus, the kingdom, according to these parables, was proclaimed to be present in the common experiences of that familiar milieu.

These images of the kingdom of God include ten maidens (Mt 25:1), a merchant in search of fine pearls (Mt 13:45), and the objects that a child desires (Lk 18:17). This pluralism of referents to the kingdom of God indicates that the kingdom cannot be identified exclusively with any one referent.

The kingdom of God is a tensive symbol. Tensive symbols are to be distinguished from steno symbols.

Steno symbols are used to indicate a distinctive referent in a one-to-one correlation. For example, Joan of Arc is identified by the steno symbol of the lark.

On the other hand, tensive symbols can never be limited to any one referent, nor to a collection of referents. Rather, tensive symbols have more symbolic values than human imagination can fashion. The parables' use of a great many referents for the kingdom of God indicates that the author of the parables had proclaimed the kingdom of God to be present in a great many circumstances and occurrences. Therefore, the author of the parables intended the kingdom to be a tensive symbol, i.e., it refers to more events than can be exhausted by the human imagination.

This identification of the kingdom of God not only as a symbol but more specifically as a tensive symbol is of critical importance. It contributes to the enriching evolution of the modern reinterpretation of the phrase "kingdom of God" that began with Johannes Weiss' proposal that the phrase was an apocalyptic concept.

Norman Perrin moved that reinterpretation forward to what he considered to be a temporary resolution with his perception that the kingdom of God is a tensive symbol. The resolution to which he referred was the emerging perception that the kingdom of God is not a concept; in place of tracing the kingdom of God to a single referent, such as the church, persons are able to discern an endless number of referents that suggest receding reaches of meaning. The kingdom of God, symbolic in a tensive manner, is present in more situations than can be exhausted by any one referent or even by any series of referents. The kingdom of God is to be understood as a symbol which evokes a myth of God acting as king among human persons in every circumstance.

However, in order for the human imagination to entertain this myth, it must be responsive to symbolic meanings. C.H. Dodd had discovered this in the parables' presumption that their listeners respond to symbols. Listeners were presumed to respond with a mind that was open to the subtle nuances of all the references to the kingdom of God.

Such nuances can be distinguished in three different references to the kingdom: (a) the kingdom sayings, (b) the Lord's prayer as expressed in Luke 11:2–4, and (c) the proverbial sayings that need to be considered along with the parables.

There are at least five kingdom sayings:

(1) "But if it is by the finger of God that I cast out demons, then the kingdom of God has come upon you" (Lk 11:20). Luke's Jesus is defending his exorcising of evil spirits. This kingdom saying proclaims that the kingdom has already come, that God is already acting as king not only in an image, but as an historical

event occurring in the experience of healing within human community. This active presence of God is proclaimed as extended throughout the human community; it is proclaimed by Luke to extend even to experiences removed at some distance in time from Jesus' behaviors and relationships. Luke, writing his proclamation of the kingdom at least two generations after the death of Jesus, announced the kingdom to be present long after Jesus had died.

(2) "When Jesus was asked by the Pharisees when the kingdom of God was coming, he answered them 'The kingdom of God is not coming with signs to be observed; nor will they say, 'Lo, here it is!' or 'There!' for behold, the kingdom of God is in the midst of you'"(Lk 17:20–21).

This saying reflects the parables' tensive use of the symbol "the kingdom of God." This kingdom saying denies explicitly that there can be a single referent for the kingdom. The kingdom is not to be identified with any one sign or institution or historical expression of an institution, not with signs here or there. The author of this kingdom saying directed attention to God's presence, but not to specific signs indicating that presence.

Though this turn away from any one sign as manifesting the kingdom may appear to remove the kingdom from sense experience, it affirms the ubiquitousness of the location of the kingdom. The person with an open mind will be able to discern traces of that presence in surprising situations, even if there are no univocal signs that identify the kingdom with concrete historical events or institutions.

(3) "The Pharisees came and began to argue with him, seeking from him a sign from heaven, to test him. And he sighed deeply in his spirit, and said, 'Why does this generation seek a sign? Truly, I say to you, no sign shall be given to this generation'" (Mk 8:11–12).

How different such an attitude is from Augustine's thesis, repeated by too many churchmen, in his referring to the church as the kingdom. The author of this saying, rather than developing a reasoned demonstration that an event is the kingdom, rather than directing attention to signs that convince the human mind of that presence, rather than offering a documented historical establishment of this kingdom, refuses to treat the presence of God as though it were a sensuous, empirical datum. God is present to persons in the manner neither of physical objects nor of institutional events that can be interpreted unequivocally.

(4) "From the days of John the Baptist until now the kingdom of heaven has suffered violence, and men of violence take it by force" (Mt 11:12).

The author of this saying refers to the kingdom by citing the deaths of John the Baptist and of Jesus. These deaths were being cited as signs which evoked for the early Christian community the myth of God acting as king in the midst of the community. In these deaths, i.e., in the violence suffered by the kingdom of God, the community was to understand that the presence of God was engaged in a struggle with powers of evil in an eschatological conflict. In that conflict the presence of God does not displace evil from the midst of humanity. However, the community is urged to believe that God is active within evil and tragedy. Just as the presence of God in the deaths of Jesus and of John was victorious over death, so that presence is victorious in other human violence, e.g., in human envy, jealousy, prejudice, nationalism, or war.

This saying, as the previous two sayings, colors the significance of the kingdom of God in shadings which might not be expected. Some persons can assume that the presence of God in our midst always emerges as clearly and conventionally victorious over evil. However, the image of this saying envisions the presence of God as active precisely within experiences of violent defeat and tragic suffering, not only in the murders of Jesus and John, but in the failures of all believers. Amidst these evils in the human community God can appear to limp. However, the kingdom of God is acknowledged by this saying to be tensively present: God's present activity is not manifest in the anticipated victory. The kingdom of God has such a complexity of referents that God is as present in defeats, tragedies, and failures as in victories and successes.

(5) "Father, hallowed be thy name. Thy kingdom come. Give us each day our daily bread; and forgive us our sins, for we ourselves forgive every one who is indebted to us; and lead us not into temptation" (Lk 11:2–4).

"Thy kingdom" in this prayer is yet another use of the kingdom of God as a tensive symbol. The tensive use of the symbol is evident in the psychology of a community at common prayer. The meanings of the words of a communal prayer vary from one person to another. Luke presented this prayer for use by all members of the believing community. The kingdom is the center of focus in this common prayer; thus, Luke accepts as valid the pluralism of referents to the kingdom of God that occurs to those who offer this prayer.

Furthermore, there are three petitions in the prayer: (i) the supplication for daily bread, (ii) the request for forgiveness, and (iii) the plea that those who pray not be led into temptation. These can be understood to indicate some of the human experiences in which God acts as king in persons' lives. Yet these three experiences do not exhaust the manner in which God so acts. On the contrary, the listing of three petitions suggests that there are many ways in which God might be expected to exercise his kingly activity among humans. There are too many such activities to identify in a prayer.

These New Testament "kingdom sayings" offer evidence that the synoptics used "the kingdom of God" as a tensive symbol.

There is in the New Testament, as well, a scattering of sayings that can be identified as the proverbial sayings. Several of these provide further identification of the manner in which the kingdom of God is present. In fact, such sayings provide what might be considered to be the most clear indicators, not of specific referents, but of the kind of experiences in which persons can expect to encounter the presence and activity of God.

Although not all of these sayings refer explicitly to the kingdom of God, their oblique references to the kingdom suggest a need to revise the understanding of the manner in which God is present in human experience. They proclaim that human experience has been radically changed by the presence of the kingdom.

There are at least four distinct kinds of these sayings. The most radical of these are from Luke and Matthew:

"Leave the dead to bury their own dead; but as for you, go and proclaim the kingdom of God" (Lk 9:60).

"But I say to you, do not resist one who is evil. But if anyone would sue you and take your coat, let him have your cloak as well; and if anyone forces you to go one mile, go with him two miles" (Mt 5:39–41).

Such radical sayings shatter any assumption that the human life of the believer is to be ordered and convenient.

The first saying is concerned not with the burial of the dead, the second neither with the sharing of garments nor with traveling with someone who forces others to march. Though they express such directives, they are actually directing their hearers to question themselves radically. They intend to jolt their hearers out of the human effort to make a continuous whole out of existence. They proclaim that God's activity as king in our midst breaks apart that which humans consider to be integrated living.

There are also eschatological reversal sayings. These are in Mark's gospel:

"For whoever would save his life will lose it; and whoever loses his life for my sake and the gospel's will save it"(Mk 8:35).

"And Jesus looked around and said to his disciples, 'How hard it will be for those who have riches to enter the kingdom of God! . . . It is easier for a camel to go through the eye of a needle than for a rich man to enter the kingdom of God'" (Mk 10:23–25).

Such sayings are identified as "eschatological reversal sayings" to indicate the challenge of the symbol, "the kingdom." God's presence in the human community summons believers to reverse values that culture expects them to embrace. The sayings are concerned not with the losing or saving of life, nor with a camel's going through the eye of a needle, but with conventional values. Those who accept the kingdom as present in their midst are summoned to reexamine the values which human convention uses to assess experience and to be open to the value of embracing the reversal of those values.

Conflict sayings are the third kind of maxims that identify the meaning of the kingdom of God.

The conflict maxim in Mark's gospel is situated within a confrontation between Jesus and scribes from Jerusalem. The scribes are questioning Jesus about his power to cast out demons. Mark's gospel there (Mk 2:27) portrays Jesus as insisting that the kingdom indeed is in the midst of the people. He is portrayed as arguing that, because of the presence of the kingdom, he is able to exercise authority over evil spirits.

"But no one can enter a strong man's house and plunder his goods, unless he first binds the strong man; then, indeed, he may plunder his house" (Mk 3:27).

This conflict saying proclaims that God is active within the human community even in experiences of conflict. Conflicts, which will be resolved eschatologically, are the tensions between forces resisting God's presence within the human community and the presence of God breaking into the human community; they occur at times in perilous circumstances. This conflict saying urges its hearers to remain confident during such peril that God is, indeed, actively confronting the resisting forces.

The parenetical maxims are the fourth and last kind of proverbial sayings. Sayings are "parenetical," a word derived from the Greek word "paraenesis," meaning "exhortation," "advice," or "counsel," because they offer counsels of wisdom to those who intend to live in the kingdom of God.

"No one who puts his hand to the plow and looks back is fit for the kingdom of God" (Lk 9:62).

"Judge not, that you be not judged. For with the judgment you pronounce you will be judged, and the measure you give will be the measure you get" (Mt 7:1–2).

Such parenetical wisdom exhorts persons to structure personal responses to experience in such a manner that they respond always to the presence of the kingdom of God, not to self-concerns. Persons are to seek to discover the linkages between all experiences and the kingdom of God. The wisdom in these sayings urges the hearers to trust in the presence of the kingdom, to tolerate the inconveniences that will be required in trusting in the kingdom, and to be patient in allowing God as king to act in his own paradoxical ways.

The forms of proclamation of the presence of the kingdom of God are thus located in parables, proverbial sayings, and radical sayings. In these the authors of the New Testament presented the symbol of the kingdom of God without referring to a univocal sign that identifies the kingdom. Nor is the kingdom envisioned as reserved in a sacred space, but rather as distributed throughout the human community. Therefore, the proclamations deliberately avoided referring to sacred spaces, events, or institutions as the reserved places in which the kingdom is present.

Furthermore, the New Testament authors proposed that the kingdom of God is to be found in a range of experiences, including experiences of conflict. Those who rely upon the presence of the kingdom are to acknowledge conflict as a paradoxical presence of the kingdom. Conflict can be a sign that God as king is reversing such values as the security which human convention endorses. Those who rely upon the presence of the kingdom thus need to be sensitive to traces of the kingdom and to respond to such traces within the human community. The proclamation of the presence of this kingdom confronts its hearers with the crisis of committing themselves wholly to a new world-view.

However, the Christian tradition that formed itself around the New Testament modified the proclamation of the kingdom of God. In place of focusing upon the presence of the kingdom of

God, Christianity focused upon the belief in a salvation effected by Jesus Christ and the eschatological resolution of cosmic tension in a future coming of the Son of Man. The paschal event of Christ Jesus had drawn the attention of believers away from the proclamation to the proclaimer, Christ Jesus. Thus the early Christians altered their focus. They turned their attention to the person of the Christ who had inspired their faith in the universal presence of God. Thus, they fashioned Christian faith in terms of belief in Christ Jesus. Moreover, they consequently altered the New Testament's focal kerygma of the presence of God in the midst of the human community. Their focus became the practices manifesting their belief in Christ's presence, i.e., practices of trust in Christ, prayer, table-fellowship, and service to the needs of others.

This modifying of the object of focus for the Christian kerygma has been most significant. The kerygma that emerged from the apostolic age determined both the form of faith in Jesus Christ and the themes to be used in Christian preaching. The degree to which the original form of the kerygma had changed can be noted in the infrequency of Christian preaching's attention either to the myth of the kingly activity of God within the human community or to the tensive symbol of the kingdom of God. In place of these, preaching has attended first to a hope that the Son of Man will come again to resolve the problem of the salvation of the cosmos, then to an interpretation of God as present in the hierarchical church.

However, it would be inappropriate to criticize these modifications and their consequent doctrines by dismissing those reinterpretations by the earliest Christians. Persons who live at a distance of almost two thousand years from those first generations of Christians are not in a position to appreciate the psychological situation in which they had lived and which had motivated them to act as they did. Therefore, modern Christians would be acting in a narrow and prejudiced manner if they rejected the alterations of the kerygma which the early Christians introduced.

It is, however, appropriate to consider a method by which to apply the original kerygma of the New Testament to the present culture. Such a consideration leads to the need to discover a heuristic for the New Testament.

Heuristics are systems for studying objects, for questioning them, for discovering their meaning, and for applying what is learned. A consideration of the kingdom of God needs a heuristic by which persons might discover the initial meaning of the kingdom of God and the means by which they might attempt to apply that symbol to the present culture.

This heuristic must include questions to be directed toward the belief in the kingdom of God. Among these questions is a probe to learn how human experience might be modified by the presence of the kingdom of God within experience.

Nevertheless, many persons will refuse to entertain such a probe insofar as they are reluctant to surrender their learned understandings of human life. Each person has expended effort to interpret experience; this learned interpretation provides a degree of security in understanding the world in the manner that is adequate for living. It is too difficult for some persons to open themselves to a reinterpretation of experience which might lead to values and meanings that seem to be alien. However, the presence of the kingdom of God just so challenges each person to put aside the interpretations aleady learned and the consequent personal security. Such a challenge is much more than a request for a modification of behavior; it is a challenge to adopt a new world-view. Those who have a fragile self-image or who are insecure about being socially acceptable might not be able to adapt themselves to a radically new world-view. Thus, to the degree that the world-view of the kingdom departs significantly from the conventional world-view, to that degree fewer persons might be willing to adapt themselves to the kingdom.

The conventional world-view of the west proposes as the criteria for meaning such standards as logic, consistency, and systematic ordering. Westerners therefore can be expected to be able to approach experience only with a degree of logic, consistency, and systematic understanding.

However, if the kerygma proposes that there is a better interpretation than that which is accepted by western culture, then persons sensitive to culture will immediately demand that the kerygmatic proposal be examined to determine whether or not it is valid. If the proposal appears to diverge from the criteria of culture, then it is unreasonable to expect participants in culture to be able to adopt the proposed world-view.

This human reluctance to be open to new ways of interpreting experience is critical. Openness is required by the kerygma of the New Testament; the kerygma challenges persons to locate their security not in their present relationships with the world, but in the presence of God announced in the kerygma. The kingdom of God is the worldly presence of God in every experience, where God acts to provide to each person that which is for one's good. Consequently, persons need to locate their security not in conventional secular values, but in the announced presence.

Conversely, the desire to acquire such secular values as greater consumption, deterministic quantities, or invulnerability, however well respected these might be in contemporary western culture, might be at odds with the activity of God within experience. Yet, the New Testament urges persons to trust in God, not in securities. Thus, they are challenged to be less attached to those values that appear to be obstacles to a response to the presence of God.

However, this reflection upon a new world-view's interpretation of experience or a new heuristic will appear to be premature at this point in the essay. Before persons can adopt a new heuristic, they need some evidence that such a modification in their method of discovering meaning is required.

The search for such evidence begins in this essay with a reflection upon God as present in the human community and as acting there as king. The meaning of this presence is a new world-view.

The world has already been considered from the new world-view of contemporary physics; there has already been a refashioning of the meanings that convention and common sense have discovered. A new vista has appeared; it can open persons to new interpretations of the world and new possibilities emerging upon the horizon.

The new world-view of the kingdom can similarly open persons to new dimensions within human consciousness. The new world-view of physics is available to those who respect the developments within physics. The world-view of the kingdom is available to those who respect the testimony of those persons, such as Jesus and the authors of the New Testament, who have glimpsed traces of the kingdom within the world.

These persons propose the need for a new perspective from which to interpret experience. Those who attend to such a proposal are challenged either to be open to the implied revelation of new meanings or to withdraw by choosing to interpret experience from only their present perspective.

Openness to the possibility of a new perspective is thus a heuristic for the kingdom of God. If God is present and active in this world, then those who claim to believe this need to be open to adopt a new perspective from which to view the divine activity. They cannot both believe in the kingdom and be skeptical and suspicious about the possibility of anything in experience that is unexpected.

This heuristic for the kingdom is also a heuristic with which to reflect upon God. "God" designates the divine person who is dynamic in the world. God's being so dynamic may be wholly different from all human dynamics; thus, the activity of God can be expected to be quite other in purpose and in pattern than the activity of humans. Thus, for example, because human activity strives to be logical, God's wholly different activity is expected not to be logical. Human logic urges persons to seek victory in strength; the divine logic of the cross seeks victory in weakness. The divine activity manifests a-logical purposes. Similarly, because human activity strives to be rational, God's activity is expected to be non-rational. Nor need the divine activity fit into any other of the forms which are criteria for valued human activities.

The activity of God can be expected to be so far removed from human orientations that logic, reason, and systems of thought may fail to provide any clue concerning the operations of God. Therefore, those who believe that the Presence (of God) is active within their experiences need to become open to the wholly unexpected purposes and activities of this Presence. Those who are open only to activities which fall within the range of secularly endorsed criteria will be blind to the Presence. A heuristic of the Presence, as a heuristic of contemporary physics, is openness.

Along with this, the believer needs to live with the heuristic of choosing to risk being vulnerable. This is a consequence of openness. The person who has chosen to be open to the unexpected cannot remain attached to the securities of life. Such a person has chosen, rather, to be willing to risk the insecurity that results from placing self within the values resulting from unexpected dimensions within experience. The resulting novel values might lead a person to venture away from prior values and their securities. They might lead along unknown paths, even paths that require a person to act in manners that convenience would prefer to reject.

The believer who has chosen so to be open to a new worldview and so to risk personal vulnerability has trusted that the world is good. He trusts thus because of his confidence in the

Presence that is active everywhere within the world. Because this trustworthy Presence is in every experience, the world is consequently good. Thus, this believer can face the world with a trust and a hope that are responses to the belief in the Presence.

This trust in the goodness of the Presence in the midst of the world allows the believer to regard with hope the cultural developments that take place as history unfolds. There need be in such a believer no fear in the face of such developments as increasing secularization or expanding liberalization of social mores. Because the Presence is functioning within the dynamics of the world's cultures, the shifts in culture's values can be trusted to be, at least in part, manifestations of the activity of the Presence in the midst of the human community.

Along with openness and vulnerability, the third element of a heuristic for the kingdom of God is a moral stance toward society. This element of the heuristic follows from the belief that the Presence is active throughout the human community. Hence, if God is active in any person's experiences, then God is active in every person's experiences. The proclamation of the New Testament authors is that "the kingdom of God is in your midst." This "your" is understood to refer to all human communities. Thus, the New Testament authors proclaimed that the Presence of the kingdom of God is active wherever there are humans. Such a plotting of the locations of the kingdom locates the Presence as distributed wherever humans exist.

The faith that the kingdom of God is actively present among all persons implies that society's ethical standards need to be modified. Persons ought not principally be acquisitive of society's goods, but rather free from the need to search for security and recognition. The social value in being free from the self-concern of acquiring goods is that persons can then live with a concern for all persons, rather than for themselves. Rather than seeking for their own security, rather than trying to insure themselves against the insecurities of the future, believers can direct themselves into the future with their eyes upon others and with the confidence that the Presence is working for everyone there in the future.

Such a hope is liberating; the trust that unexpected and fertile opportunities of living will be offered by the Presence liberates persons from the need to search for securities. Persons can hope that unexpected opportunities will be made available to all who live in the kingdom of God. Because they believe that the

Presence will always be active, they can rely vulnerably upon the Presence in every event and every person that the future will introduce to them.

The focus of the chapter shifts at this point. The chapter's first two objectives were to present the New Testament's proclamation of the kingdom of God and to propose the heuristic for interpreting that proclamation and applying it to human praxis. Now the focus shifts to consider the third objective: to identify the direction in which persons need to orient themselves in order to be disposed to interact with the Presence within experiences. Persons need an appropriate orientation if they are going to allow God to act as king in their lives.

This orientation is developed in the parables of the New Testament. Thus, this manuscript now returns to a consideration of the parables of the evangelists; however, this turning to the parables is distinct from the earlier reflection. Earlier the concern was to identify the content of the kerygma; namely, that the kingdom of God is in the midst of the human community. The symbol of the kingdom of God was then recognized as intending to evoke the myth of God's active presence in the common experiences of the world, where God functions as king. However, this turn to the parables is intended to identify the orientation required of persons if they are to discover evidences of the kingdom of God in the world of human consciousness.

The parables as a body of literature can appear to be problematic; they do not immediately appear to express an integrating theme. Thus, in an effort to introduce some elementary categories under which the parables can be grouped, this chapter will begin its discussion by focusing upon three key parables that manifest structures of behavior that can be found in a majority of the parables. These three key parables are (a) the hidden treasure (Mt 13:44), (b) the pearl of great price (Mt 13:45–46), and (c) the dragnet thrown into the sea (Mt 13:47–50). This third parable is found in a more developed form in the Gospel according to Thomas (Thomas 81:20–82:3).[5]

The first two structure a sequence of behaviors which can serve as a model orientation for those who hope to respond to the experience of the kingdom of God. (1) The man who finds the object of his quest has found a trace of the kingdom, i.e., the treasure; (2) he then sells or disposes of all that he has as now of little value i.e., he assesses all other values to be subordinate to the value of the kingdom; (3) finally he buys or acquires the object which he recognizes as the treasure. This structured sequence can be discussed in the more general terms of advent–reversal–action. "Advent" signifies that the encounter with the kingdom or the Presence disorients a person from the normal patterns of life. "Reversal" signifies that this encounter can lead a person to reverse his past manner of evaluating life. "Action" signifies that the person who has encountered an experience of the kingdom and has revised his priorities goes on to act in a manner that he would otherwise not have acted.

This sequence can be observed in the key parables.

(1) "The kingdom of heaven is like treasure hidden in a field, which a man found and covered up; then in his joy he goes and sells all that he has and buys that field" (Mt 13:44).

This very brief parable suggests the attraction of the kingdom in the advent–reversal–action pattern. The advent moment from the structure of behaviors is expressed in the parable in the comparison of the kingdom to treasure. The discovery of a treasure connotes that the encounter with the kingdom is a most positive experience. When a person discovers a treasure, he spontaneously desires to hold it fast. A discovered treasure is attractive enough to occupy all of the concern of the person who discovers it. This response is indicated in the parable by the interior action of the joy because of having come upon the treasure and the joy that leads to covering up the treasure in an effort to secure it.

The reversal moment in the pattern is manifest in the response of the man to the treasure. He does what is extraordinary in order to lay claim to the find. Because he evaluates the treasure as more valuable than all that he has, he revises his priorities so as to secure possession of the treasure; he "sells all that he has" or reverses his entire past manner of evaluating life.

The third moment in the structure is illustrated in the man's decision to buy the field. The discovery of a genuine treasure by a person attracts the entire concentration and commitment of the discoverer, leads the person to revise his priorities, and then attracts the person so to act as to secure possession of the treasure. This action generally takes the form of a commitment and a risk. Thus, in this parable the man took the risk of selling all that he had; he then made a commitment by investing his all in order to lay claim to the field that held the treasure.

(2) "Again, the kingdom of heaven is like a merchant in search of fine pearls, who, on finding one pearl of great value, went and sold all that he had and bought it" (Mt 13:45–46).

This second key parable manifests the same structure of behavior: advent–reversal–action. The difference is that now the object of attraction is the pearl that satisfies the man who had been seeking marketable pearls. The similarity is that the object of attraction came into the merchant's life and attracted the same response as the buried treasure had. In this parable, as in the previous one, the one who found the treasure sold all that he had in order to secure possession of the prized discovery. Such a response to the advent of an object of attraction exemplifies the reversal moment in the structure of behavior that is appropriate for an encounter with traces of the kingdom. In an encounter with the object of one's desire the person will likely invert his priorities in order to risk committing himself to that which has been found. All the security that had previously been located in "all that he had" is risked in the transfer to the object that has been found, i.e., to the treasure, to the pearl, or to the encounter with the kingdom of God.

(3a) "Again, the kingdom of heaven is like a net which was thrown into the sea and gathered fish of every kind; when it was full, men drew it ashore and sat down and sorted the good into vessels but threw away the bad" (Mt 13:47–48).

This parable repeats again the advent–reversal–action pattern that had been exemplified in the previous parables. The good fish attracted the attention of the fishermen; he selected the good fish as his catch and discarded the others. However, these discarded fish would have been kept if "the good fish" had not been in the net.

This parable appears in another form in the Gospel according to Thomas

(3b) "And he said: the man is like a wise fisherman who cast his net into the sea, he drew it up from the sea full of small fish; among them he found a large, good fish, that wise fisherman; he threw all the small fish down into the sea, he chose the large fish without regret. Whoever has ears to hear let him hear" (Thomas 81:24–82:3).[6]

In the parable the fisherman catches a large, good fish; because it is such an unexpected, prize catch, he discards all the other fish, which, though good, were smaller. The advent of the large fish opened up a new priority of values for the man. The new value was a catch so good that the rest of his valuables no longer appeared to be comparable. Thus, he inverted his priorities. Rather than keeping all the fish in his boat, "he threw all the small fish down into the sea." As in the previous parables, so in this, the one who finds the treasure responds to his discovery with risk and commitment. The priority of values in his previous fishing had been to take as many fish as he was able to bring into his boat. However, when he catches the large, good fish, he inverts these priorities. In place of keeping the many fish, as he generally had, the fisherman now keeps only the one large fish.

The kingdom of God is identified in each of these three parables as a value so attractive that, when it comes into a person's life (advent), the person is portrayed as reversing his previous ways of evaluating life and taking the action of risking everything in order to experience the kingdom.

These are the parables which can be identified as the key to the themes found in the other parables. They are paradigms or referent parables that demonstrate the appropriate behaviorial response to an encounter with a trace of the kingdom of God. The person who has such an encounter is encouraged by these parables to dispose himself toward the kingdom in this pattern.

There are, of course, other parables which might be considered in the search for the proper orientation in encountering traces of the kingdom of God.

The parable of the sower deserves some consideration. Although there is no reason to turn to this rather than to another parable, it is a parable that illumines the path along which to travel in the hope of properly orienting oneself toward the kingdom of God.

The parable begins quite simply.

"Listen! A sower went out to sow. And as he sowed, some seed fell along the path, and the birds came . . ." (Mk 4:3).

The kingdom is not mentioned in the narration; yet the parable proposes attitudes appropriate for an extraordinary dimension of life's experience. These attitudes can be discovered in considering the contrast between the infertility of the seed on the path, on the rocks, and among the thorns, and the fertility of that which fell on good soil.

The core of the parable is the overly abundant fertility of the seed that fell on good soil: thirty-, sixty- and a hundredfold. Those familiar with farming know that seed is not so fertile. Thus, the parable climaxes with the surprising fertility. The appropriate human attitude toward experience is this surprise. The parable is concerned not with the meager growth of the other seed, but with the surprising growth of the last seed. It is a parable about the surprising presence of the kingdom as an unexpected presence within experience.[7]

The attitude proposed to persons hoping to discover the kingdom of god in human experience is a sensitivity to the surprise of life. Such an attitude is illumined by its foil, the blasé disinterest exhibited by persons who assume that there is nothing new in human experience, no possibility of a numinous encounter. The parable of the sower cautions its hearers against being so disposed toward life that they expect no surprises or that they fail to respond to them. The positive response toward surprise within experience that the parable encourages is an access to the Presence actively transforming human lives.

Conversely, persons who refuse to identify the surprises in life or who insist that whatever occurs must be explainable in material causes only are, in the world-view of the parable, not likely to discover the kingdom in their midst.

The parable of the good Samaritan is another illustration of the same attitude, i.e., the disposition that allows persons to discover encounters with the kingdom of God in their midst (Lk 10:30–37). The narration tells of a man, presumably a Jew, who, going down from Jerusalem to Jericho, fell among robbers. The robbers stripped the man, beat him, and left him half dead. Later a priest, also a Jew, journeyed along the same road, saw the beaten man, but passed him by. Similarly, a Levite, a member of the Jewish priestly association that minister in the sanctuary, journeyed along the road, saw the man, but passed on without attending to the victim. Then one of those despised and abused by Jews, a Samaritan, came by, saw him, had compassion upon him, and ministered to him in every way in which he was able.

The surprising twist in the parable is the image of the care given by the Samaritan, not by the priest nor by the Levite, to the Jewish victim of the beating. This reverses the expected images of Jewish culture. Those addressed by the parable, i.e., Jewish people, were accustomed to regard priests and Levites as fellows, and Samaritans as worthless and despicable. However, the parable not only presents a Samaritan who was a neighbor to the unfortunate Jew, but also the two priestly Jews as ignoring the plight of the victim, their fellow Jew. Expectations were reversed. Such a reversal proposes an inversion of priorities: all persons, even Samaritans, can be neighbors; those whom Jews despise, e.g., the Samaritan, can be more loving to their antagonists than those whom Jews admire and respect, e.g. the priest and the Levite.

This parable, in a manner not dissimilar from that of the parables of the sower, the hidden treasure, the pearl of great value, and the great fish, directs its hearers to seek the kingdom of God in situations which reverse conventional values: the despised Samaritan can be of great worth, can be even morally superior to Jewish priests and Levites. Experiences of the kingdom are to be expected just there where priorities are inverted. God is to be expected to shatter human assumptions and expectations.

The parable of the vineyard workers (Mt 20:1–13) presents a similar theme. It is a narration about a householder who hires laborers to work in his vineyard. At four different times during the working day the householder goes out to hire laborers. However, when he pays these workers, he pays them all with the wage that he had pledged to those who had been hired at the beginning of the day. This distribution of wages on the basis of generosity reverses the expectations of all of the laborers. The laborers who had worked all day had expected to receive more; those who had worked less expected less.

Again, the parable urges persons to be disposed to find the Presence of God not where they expect it, but where they least expect it.[8] These poetic metaphors summon persons to live with an awareness that there is in human experiences a dynamic that is subtly elusive, i.e., that can too easily be ignored unless one is disposed to respond to surprises.[9]

To live with an openness to the Presence, however, is possible only for those who risk participating in life with those attitudes proposed in the poetic metaphors of the parables. The world envisioned by these metaphors suggests the world of Israel in the first century. The activities and personality types of that world were familiar to the hearers of the parables.

Nonetheless, even contemporary persons can be open to the Presence active in the world as presented by the metaphors. That Presence is anticipated as active even in the inversion of the values, the assumptions, and the meanings within the common-sense world of human conventions. Even the contemporary hearers of the parables are thus invited to regard their experiences with a fresh view. They are urged to orient themselves to the Presence active within the world. They are asked to be conscious of those entirely new dimensions in human life that the Presence introduces. Finally, they are asked to be so disposed toward their experiences as to focus upon the kingdom of God as present within the unexpected occurrences of their lives.

The parables urge persons to trust that God is active as king in the human community. However, they also caution persons against using common sense to assume that humans know how God acts. God is actively present in surprising manners. Thus, humans would be foolish to presume that the Presence acts only conventionally within human consciousness and the human community. On the contrary, because the kingdom of God emerges in situations and in relationships which are inversions of conventional situations and relationships, there is need for persons to be open to surprisingly new manners of relating to the world. Thus, only those who are positively oriented to variety and surprise can be open to the Presence in their midst. In order so to be open, persons cannot expect human life to be a continuous whole. Conversely, persons are challenged by the kerygma of the kingdom to expect life for the believer to be discontinuous with the conventional life of surrounding culture. They are, therefore, to be vulnerable in their openness. They may thus appear in the opinion of non-believers to be out of step with the values and behaviors of culture.[10]

For example, some are urged by the Presence to trust others generally or to avoid using any defensive devices in their relationships; such persons are likely to find that their lives are frequently shattered, i.e., their lives are not likely to be continuous wholes. On the other hand, there are persons who choose to shield their lives from any dynamic which might fracture their security. These persons are more cautious and defensive.

The human advantage of openness is that it orients persons to discover the unexpected values within the surprises of life.

Persons who believe that the kingdom of God is present might be willing to allow the Presence to shatter the accustomed patterns of their lives and to restructure their choices. They can so respond because they trust that in surprises God is acting as king in unexpected but favorable ways. Therefore, the choices that had come to be conventional and expected are allowed to be shattered by the Presence and are dismissed by persons in order that new paths and new dimensions might be fashioned for the believer by the Presence.

The kerygma of the kingdom of God has thus been positioned. First of all the meaning of the kingdom of God was derived from the New Testament texts. The symbol of the kingdom in the New Testament was recognized to refer to a multiplicity of referents. That symbol directs attention to the multiple ways in which one is to believe that God acts in the midst of the human community. Conversely, there is no one referent which exhausts the meaning of God's activity within the human community. Within human consciousness and human experience God is active in more ways than human wisdom can comprehend. Thus, God's active presence has in this essay been referred to by the non-referential noun, the "Presence."

Second, a heuristic of the Presence was developed. Because Christians believe that God is actively present in the human community, they can use a method of discerning evidence of his presence and activity within the world. The chapter therefore derived a relationship between the kingdom of God and human experience. It concluded that the bridge between humans and the kingdom of God is a human openness to life, a vulnerability to the risks involved in being so open, and sensitivity to social justice.

Openness is a heuristic that follows from trusting that God is active in the surprising occurrences within the experiences of human community. Thus, in order to interact with God's surprising actions, a person needs to remain pliable to the implications which occur in experience.

Vulnerability is a heuristic that follows from being genuinely open. The open person is one who allows himself to become involved in situations and relationships in which security might become fragile. The open person is willing to live without securities and is willing to expose himself to whatever he finds in his milieu. Thus, he is vulnerable.

A heuristic of the moral posture toward society follows from the belief that God is acting everywhere in the midst of the community. Because there is no place in society from which God is absent, then God is to be understood as active in every part of society. Thus, every person can expect God to be extending to him the divine care and concern. Furthermore, believers are to translate God's universal care into the moral posture of being positively disposed to everyone. Believers are therefore to endorse a social care for all persons in the human community. Thus, believers will collaborate with this concern by promoting equal justice for every person.

Third, the orientations or dispositions required to discover the kingdom of God within experience were developed. To derive these the chapter turned again to the parables of the New Testament. These announce that the kingdom of God, active upon the earth, can be encountered by persons who adopt certain dispositions. Among these dispositions are a responsiveness modeled upon the advent–reversal–action pattern of behavior, a willingness to explore surprises, and an openness to experiences which shatter human understandings and conventions. The New Testament proclaims that in all experiences, especially those that are unconventional, God might very well be acting as king to fashion surprisingly new values for persons in the world. God invites persons to choose these fresh values within experience.

The kingdom of God thus takes not a definite form, but lies before a definite orientation. The heuristic with which to discover the kingdom in the midst of the human community enables persons to orient themselves toward the Presence.

This essay has discerned a harmony between the presences discovered in research by contemporary physics and the Presence of the New Testament. Western culture thus can put aside some of its skepticism concerning the Presence.

However, in order to discern that harmony there is a need at this point to reflect upon the manner in which contemporary physics is understood to converge with the New Testament proclamation. There is a need to defend the language that this essay has used to argue that there is a similarity between the presences of physics and the Presence of the New Testament.

5

....

Homer, Einstein, Darwin, and Bach

The confluence of these four names might appear at first to result in a swirl of conflicting values and interests. The great epic poet, the founder of contemporary physics, the discoverer of evolution, and the great baroque musical composer seem to belong in quite discrete categories. However, they are here brought together in a theological monograph in order to illumine the path along which theological reflection passes.

The creative mind articulates itself. The goal of creative thinking is not empirically to describe objective matter that can be encountered. Rather, the creative thinking person reaches into the mind and grasps the mind's understanding of an experience. Creative thinking turns then to reflect upon that understanding. Ultimately the creative person articulates that understanding in a form that communicates the meaning that the mind has fashioned.

Meaning appears within the mind not as a result of accurately picturing an experience, but as a consequence of a starburst of intuitive imagination. Homer had not accurately described the objective lives of Priam, Achilles, Hector, Hecuba, or Odysseus; rather, he had intuited the meaning of their lives in a burst of imagination. Nor had Einstein accurately pictured the form of the space–time of the universe; with an intuitive leap of imagination he had fabricated that form from the free play of his mind. Similarly Darwin had imagined the process of evolution to be a plausible explanation for the variations in the plant-life and animal-life that he had studied on the Galapagos Islands. So too Johann S. Bach had composed his great musical scores by expressing on paper the relationship of tones and meter that his mind had imagined.

The human Jesus of Nazareth must have used the same free play of imagination to envision the kingdom of God in the midst of the human community. By extension, those who interpret the contemporary meaning of this kingdom can do naught else but describe as accurately as they can their mind's comprehension of the meaning of that kingdom.

Whittaker Chambers, an atheistic American communist of the twentieth century, illustrated this method of interpreting the consciousness of the mind. He drew upon his imagination to fashion his belief in God. So enchanted was he with the form and power of his infant daughter's ear that he imaginatively probed his mind's grasp of experience in order to discover a source for that ear. He intuited that there must be a divine creator.[1]

The "free imaginative variation" of the human mind's grasp of experience was the phrase that Edmund Husserl had used to describe human knowledge. Knowing requires that the person bring to light the comprehension which is latent within that person's battery of imagined meanings for objective encounters within life. In every such encounter the knower seeks to discover within the mind a meaning of which the experience is an example. This search often requires the person to imagine variations of the meanings which have already been fashioned. Thus, Homer imagined the character of Achilles by free imaginative variation upon the idea of a hero; Einstein, general relativity physics by free imaginative variation upon the idea of observers in motion; Darwin, evolution by free imaginative reflection upon the idea of differences between proximate species; Jesus, the kingdom of God by free imaginative reflection upon God's gratuitous love for all persons; and Wittaker Chambers, the existence of a divine creator by free imaginative inventiveness upon the possible explanatory sources for his daughter's ear. In each case the knower seeks to describe the experience in such a manner that the experience can be understood to be an example of the idea within the actual world. Not empirical verification but imaginative comprehension is the normative light according to which one fashions one's comprehension and its consequent expression.

There is a developmental history in the human value of such imaginative knowledge.

Immanuel Kant emerges within philosophical history as the one who is credited as having explicitly recognized that human knowing is the fashioning by the mind of a description of that which appears within conscious experience.[2]

David Hume acknowledged that comprehension is a result of imaginatively interrelating the complex of concepts within the mind's resources.[3]

Georg W. F. Hegel moved the tradition further in his recognition that humans grasp not material objects but the mind as
it imaginatively encounters experience.[4]

Charles Sanders Peirce described human knowing as the creative description of whatever is before the mind.[5]

Then Edmund Husserl recognized that the intentionality of
consciousness operates universally in human knowing. That is, in
knowing, persons always intend to describe something within
consciousness. This is not an intention to verify something empirically, but to describe the ideas, concepts, and impressions with
which one encounters phenomena.[6]

Finally, in late twentieth century America David Tracy has
recognized that among the mind's resources with which it interprets any phenomenon there are religious concepts. These are no
more nor less imaginative than other sets of concepts. Just as the
physicist or the historian or the poet, so too the theologian must
imaginatively reconstruct a phenomenon with the conceptual
apparatus that is available within his or her mind.[7]

Thus, the venture proposed in this monograph fits into the
philosophical human tradition that acknowledged meaning to be
fashioned through the imaginatively structuring of the available
conceptual resources to construct a consistent world-view. A contemporary meaning of Jesus' proclamation of the kingdom of
God can be fashioned by one who uses the entire range of concepts that are accessible within the human mind. Among those
concepts is the recently fashioned world-view of contemporary
physics.

However, this essay needs to demonstrate the value of
describing experiences by articulating the concepts within the
mind's understanding of experience.

Immanuel Kant had been the most provocative spokesman
for this interpretation of human knowledge. He had proposed
that objects and events as they are in themselves can be identified
as noumena; however, human knowledge cannot grasp objects
and events as they are in themselves. Rather, the mind grasps
objects and events as they appear in human experience, i.e.,
objects and events as phenomena.

This interpretation of human knowing continues to be the
point of departure for reflection upon methods of knowing. Even
those, like Hegel, who disagree with Kant acknowledge the Kan-
tian interpretation of noumena and phenomena.

Thus, the present study will defend its conclusions by articulating a phenomenology of human knowing based upon Kant's analytic description of human knowing.

Human knowledge of phenomena is a form of intuition. Intuition is required in knowing because sense experience can grasp empirically or sensibly only noumena, not phenomena, i.e., only quantities and lines, not that which determines the identity of things. Forms, or those dynamics which make phenomena to be what they are, can be grasped only if they are imaginatively intuited. That which appears to the senses, that which can be measured empirically, is no more than quantity, movement, and line. While the quantities can be grasped by the senses, the forms that determine identities can be grasped only by a process of intuiting. The human mind needs to make an intuitive leap of imagination in order to grasp more than the quantities-in-motion which it encounters. This leap may be modest, as in grasping those quantities with which one is familiar, e.g., a sound associated with rain. Or the leap may be more dramatic, as in grasping unfamiliar sounds, e.g., an absence of sound that betokens vague tension within the environment.

In any case the mind makes its leap to understand the form only if it imagines an idea appropriate for the object encountered. This is done by the mind's filing through its known ideas in search of one of which the encountered object is an example. For example, the present study proposes that the encounter with the cosmos as understood by contemporary physics is an example of the idea of God's active Presence in the midst of the human community. This idea was proclaimed by the New Testament's "The kingdom of God is in your midst."

In order to discover whether or not the cosmos is, indeed, an example of that idea, the study needs to alter various components of the idea of the kingdom so as to discern whether in each alternative the cosmos continues to be an example of the known idea. Thus, this monograph probes to discover those components of the idea of the kingdom that are its traces. Then it seeks for those traces of the kingdom within the cosmos. To the extent that this inquiry finds such traces in the cosmos, to that extent it has discerned the cosmos to be a manifestation of the New Testament idea of the kingdom.

Among these traces of the kingdom within the cosmos is the recognition by physics that there is an abundance of non-sensuous dynamics operating within physical space–time. This suggests the kingdom of God's vision of the non-sensuous dynamic of the Presence subtly and unobservedly acting within the human community.

Another such trace is the acknowledgement by physics that there are physical dynamics which seem to operate apart from the physical restrictions under which physical dynamics normally must operate. An example of such a dynamic is the tunneling of subatomic particles out from a location in which they had been physically enclosed and isolated. This suggests the trace which is a vision of the Presence's operating according to its own, elusive patterns. In fact, the kingdom's proclamation insists that no humanly devised symbols can predict or even express the manner in which the Presence operates.

The list of such traces could continue exhaustively; one might cite the puckered form of space–time, the non-continuous and discrete quanta that form all mass-energy, or the variations in physical measurements depending upon the perspective from which motion is observed.

The plausible conclusion from the discovery of such traces is that, indeed, the physical cosmos studied by contemporary physics presents an example of the Presence of the kingdom actively working within the human environment.

Nonetheless, the person who describes the mind's comprehension of the physical cosmos as an example of the kingdom's Presence within the environment must be cautious to make no unwarranted assumptions and to describe the phenomena of the physical cosmos as they present themselves to the unbiased observer. Thus, the choice of turning to the study of contemporary physics in order to find traces of the kingdom was carefully taken: natural science demands that its phenomena be taken as science presents them. The person who seeks there for traces of the kingdom is required to describe these phenomena in just the manner that science implies that the cosmos is to be described.

Moreover, to the extent that such unbiased phenomena can be shown to be traces of examples of the idea of the kingdom, to that extent the phenomena can be persuasive that the kingdom is at least plausible as a dynamic within human experience.

In order to guard against assuming that which is to be argued, this manner of interpreting consciousness proceeds by "bracketing existence" as regards the kingdom of God. This procedure suspends belief that the cosmos is an example of the kingdom in order that a greater demand be placed upon the inquirer. He or she must begin the probe by assuming that there is no kingdom of God.

However, in the probe through the data available in the interpretation of the cosmos, the inquirer may discover traces of the kingdom. If such traces are not discerned, then the inquiry must conclude that the cosmos is not an example of the kingdom as proclaimed by the New Testament authors.

However, if the traces are uncovered, then the search for evidences of the kingdom within the cosmos can proceed to *intuit* that the kingdom is present within the cosmos as a consequence of the appropriate traces that have been glimpsed.

Nevertheless, the person who asserts that the kingdom is present must acknowledge that this assertion is possible only to the extent that one has chosen to search for traces as evidence of the kingdom. Those who choose to turn aside from such a search cannot be expected to concur with the assertion. This follows from the original purpose of the phenomenology of the interpretation–namely, to bring to light that which is latent in the intentions of a person. Only those persons who share the intention of intuitively discovering evidence of the kingdom will acknowledge the intuitive discovery of that which is latent in the consciousness of the inquiring believer. Believers can be expected to engage in the process of probing into the recesses of their consciousness for evidence of the kingdom. Of course, those who do not share this consciousness will not have available to them within their consciousness the data into which they might probe.

The convergence of Einstein and Darwin (a physicist and an evolutionist) with Homer and Bach (a poet and a music composer) was the point of departure for this chapter. The intended purpose was to suggest that natural scientists and creative artists perform activities that are most similar. At this point in the argument it is clear that these four creative thinkers had been engaged in the same enterprise–thus, the convergence. Each had articulated an imaginative interpretation of phenomena of which they were conscious. Each had been concerned to express not that which could be empirically discovered, not that which accurately described common-sense experiences, but rather their own creatively imagined consciousness of the cosmos (Einstein), of the epic grandeur of ancient heroes (Homer), of evolution (Darwin), and of the interrelationship of sounds (Bach).

The critical believer can become engaged in articulating his

or her own imaginative interpretation of one's consciousness of
the cosmos as a manifestation of the kingdom of God. Indeed,
this articulation is creatively imaginative; thus it can be situated
at the convergence of the work of the four men mentioned above.
Just as their imaginative work had been given a hearing, so this
work might deserve to be heard. Creative thought expresses the
imaginative interpretation of the contents of consciousness.

6

....

Kingdom in Cosmos

A context of nature in which to situate the kingdom of God within the world has been positioned in the four chapters on contemporary physics of this monograph. The philosophical tradition of interpreting one's consciousness of non-sensuous phenomena has been positioned in the fifth chapter. The present stage of the argument draws together those five chapters in the interpretation of the consciousess of the place of the kingdom of God within the human world.

This will be done by returning to the evidence that contemporary physics has offered to indicate that there are non-sensuous dynamics operating within the physical world. From that evidence this argument concludes that there might likely be other dynamics, not discerned by the physical sciences, which can be indications of the Presence within the world of experience.

More particularly this chapter argues that the cosmos studied by contemporary physics exemplifies the manner in which the Presence, i.e., the kingdom of God, might operate dynamically within human experience. Alternatively, the thesis to be defended is that the dynamics of the Presence are in harmony with the occurrences studied by contemporary physics.

The New Testament proclaims that the kingdom of God is in the midst of the human community, i.e., that God is present and active within the world of human experience. The authors of the New Testament proclaim as well the criteria with which one might determine that the Presence is active within the world. Yet, this Presence is not an overt dynamic; it is not clearly manifest to human perception. Thus, the God who is proclaimed to be present and active within the world must be so subtle that God is always beyond the range of that which human senses and human perception are able to grasp. Hence, there are many who conclude that the Presence is no more than a projection of hope on the part of those who choose to believe the proclamation of the New Testament.

However, contemporary physics has developed imaginative arguments which convincingly lead to the conclusion that there may be many non-empirical dynamic presences within the physical world. There dynamics, though non-sensuous, are most significant in determining the occurrences within the world. Thus, though these dynamic presences are immaterial and non-sensuous, they are critically related to all material events.

The argument of this chapter probes the convergence of these presences of contemporary physics and the Presence of the New Testament proclamation. Contemporary physicists, especially the founders of modern physics, offer a model of the kind of open mind that is required if one is to accept the possibility that the Presence is a dynamic within the world. Max Planck, Albert Einstein, Niels Bohr, Max Born, and the other pioneers of modern physics had minds open to the possibility that there are dynamic presences within the world that had been wholly unknown to classical Newtonian physicists.

Those who entertain the possibility of the Presence within the world need to have minds similarly open. They need to entertain the possibility that the dynamics of the Presence are as actual as the occurrences studied by contemporary physics, even while these dynamics of the Presence are as non-sensuous and as elusive as the occurrences studied by the physics developed in the twentieth century.

Such is the image of the form of the activity of the Presence within the world of human experience.

The light that has illumined the search for the kingdom in the cosmos is the hope to discover a path to a point of reference that acknowledges the values both of the New Testament proclamation and of the scientifically oriented culture in which westerners now live.

This point of reference would accommodate persons who are critically minded enough to question whether and how God might be present and active within a culture that appears to value only that which can be verified with certitude. The importance of such a perspective is a consequence of human temperament as a dominant influence leading the critical believer either toward faith or toward skepticism in judging the value of the Presence.

Many persons are likely to find that they are influenced by a mixture of temperaments; they are not only influenced to seek out rational explanations of the meaning of the Presence, but also to search for empirical data that either confirms or challenges the Presence. Thus, in judging whether the kingdom is in the cosmos, these persons will ask for an explanation of the New Testament ideal of the kingdom. However, they will also ask for some form of data that indicates whether the ideal of the kingdom fits harmoniously into the world of empirical knowledge.

This blend of the rationalist temperament and the empirical temperament within most westerners suggests the basis for persons' desire to discover both the scriptural explanations of the kingdom and empirical evidence with which to interpret those explanations.

The rational temperament, which William James named "the tender-minded," makes a great deal out of integrating the unity of things. In studying the kingdom in the cosmos, for example, this temperament will be pleased to rest content in the vision of the Presence as active within the human community.

However, the empirical temperament, "the tough-minded," makes a great deal out of collecting the whole of the data in order to discover inductively whether empiricism implies the Presence.

"The tender-minded" are identified by James as rationalistic, idealistic, optimistic, and religious. "The tough-minded" are empiricistic, materialistic, pessimistic, and irreligious.

Many westerners find both temperaments to be influencing their approach to judgment.[1]

The tough-minded demand an empirical basis for the Presence. Fortunately for them, the critically established conclusions of contemporary physics introduce such a foundation for the assertion of the Presence. This tough-minded search for an empirical kind of data has revealed an unexpected foundation for the tender-minded assertions about the Presence. In fact tough-minded skepticism has unexpectedly discovered that there is harmony between contemporary physics and the New Testament proclamation of the Presence. This empirical temperament has discovered that there is a startling blend of physics and the Presence. Consequently, both the rational and the empirical temperaments, i.e., both the tender-minded and the tough-minded, can find satisfaction in the search to discover whether the kingdom is located in the cosmos.

Nevertheless, if the one searching is to discover the point of reference that satisfies both temperaments, that one needs to acknowledge that the assertions of contemporary physics are

being accepted without the kind of sensuous verification and certitude that the tough-minded might presume that they should
have in their judgments. One of the purposes of the turn to contemporary physics has been to argue that sense experience and
certitude are no more important in assertions about the physical
world than they are in assertions about the Presence.

Contemporary physics envisions the physical world as the
arena of occurrences which wholly escape detection by the conventional perceptions of humans. So completely do these occurrences elude human perception that they cannot be described
precisely, but only in symbols that approximate the occurrences
that can be imagined.

Thus, physics models an openness to symbolism as the only
access to certain occurrences of the physical world. Such openness is precisely the demand that confronts those to whom the
kingdom of God is proclaimed. They are asked to assent to the
Presence that can be articulated only in symbols. The tough-
minded might initially assume that they would be naive if they
were to acknowledge that such symbols represent an actual Presence. However, the assent of modern physics to just such symbolic presences is an illustration to the tough-minded that
acknowledging such a Presence is not at all naive.

Consequently, this turning to science has identified contemporary physics as a discipline which illumines the path to be traveled by the tough-minded to whom the New Testament is proclaimed. Just as physics assents to presences within a world that
can be articulated only symbolically, so critically minded believers
might intelligently assent to the Presence that can be articulated
only symbolically. The kingdom of God might thus be envisioned
to be at least as present as the symbolic world of contemporary
physics. The Presence may be envisioned as less present, however,
to those who continue to live with the common-sense perspective
that seeks empirical certitude. There is a remarkable convergence
between the intellectual attitudes and the moral motivations of
those doing contemporary physics and those who assent to the
Presence.

This convergence has been demonstrated in the first four
chapters. The critical demand for assent to the Presence as symbolic was formulated in the fourth chapter, "The Presence: The
Kingdom of God Proclaimed."

The kingdom of God is a symbol which refers to the myth of
God active in the midst of life. Such is the meaning of the kingdom in the New Testament.

However from the time of Augustine of Hippo (died in 430 C.E.) until the beginning of the twentieth century the kingdom had been interpreted not as a symbol but as a concept. Hence the believing community had not been aware of the symbol about the myth of the Presence active among them.

Because of the current heightened awareness of the cultural value of myth, the kingdom has emerged as a symbol. Thus, the tough-minded seek to interpret that symbol by legitimately asking how they can discern the Presence within experience.

The parables of the gospels provide an initial response to this question. First of all the parables, which are generally metaphors about the kingdom of God, situate the kingdom within those life experiences that were common to those who heard the parables, e.g., common experiences such as wedding feasts, winnowing fans, threshing floors, fields in harvest, and vineyards.

Moreover, this pluralism of references to the kingdom suggests that the Presence is to be found in more situations than the human imagination can fathom. Thus, those who hope genuinely to open themselves to the kingdom will remain open to every experience, however subtle, as a possible trace of the Presence within the world. They also will be ready to respond in the manner that such traces might suggest.

However, these tough-minded will likely ask what the criteria might be that identify certain experiences as traces of the kingdom of God.

Again, the parables of the gospels provide a response. In the parables persons can find indications of the markings that identify traces of the kingdom of God within human experience.

One such criterion is the reversal of meaning or the reversal of value. As developed in the fourth chapter, such reversals suggest that the Presence is altering the meaning of human experience.

The tough-minded will find many such reversals in contemporary physics. These reversals can be interpreted to be traces of the Presence within the physical world.

Albert Einstein's special relativity physics is itself such a reversal. Einstein recognized that science had to revise the classical Newtonian standards concerning the absolute and universal validity of the measurement of objects in motion.[2]

Another New Testament criterion by which to recognize traces of the Presence is the breaking apart of the continuous whole of the order and convenience of human life. Again, the Presence is envisioned as radically altering the form of human life. Thus, as the inversion of meanings, so the breaking apart of the conventionally valued human life can be interpreted to be a trace of the Presence altering human experience.

The development first of general relativity physics, then of quantum physics opened up before those in the scientific community a chasm that indicated the breaking apart of the stable and predictable world that classical physics had predicated for three hundred years.

Einstein's general relativity physics recognized that the classical Euclidean description of objects in space had to be inaccurate: objects exist not in three-dimensional space, but in four-dimensional space–time. As a result of this drastically new world-view needed to describe objects within that framework, the conventionally valid descriptions of objects had broken apart. Thus, general relativity had discovered that the human imagination, though quite adequate for classical physics, does not have the reach that is adequate to describe objects in space–time. The human imagination has been fashioned in a world that is entirely different from the puckered world of multi-dimensional space–time.[3]

Consequently, general relativity physics has discovered the world to be an illustration of just that location which the New Testament had proposed as the situation in which to seek for traces of the Presence.

Moreover, general relativity physics can be envisioned as a paradigm of the vulnerability that the New Testament foresees as required of those who seek for the Presence in the midst of a world that is breaking apart. As a result of their drastic revisions of the world-view of physics, general relativity scientists became liable to the sometimes severe criticism of classical, Newtonian physicists. Thus, the general relativity scientists had to give up the security that they might have enjoyed if they had remained content with the stable, generally accepted world-view of Newtonian physics. However, they chose to become vulnerable to the new world-view. In doing so, they have become models of that vulnerability that the New Testament has proposed as required of those who look for traces of the Presence in the vulnerable circumstances of the breaking apart of life's conventions.

These scientists have directed the attention of modern western culture to precisely those experiences that the New Testament had proposed as criteria that indicate the traces of the activity of the Presence.

A third standard by which to discover traces of the Presence are the experienced demands made upon persons in their responding to events which lead away from the conventional logic and the closure that society identifies as marks of security. The exhortative sayings of the New Testament urge enthusiastic responses to those experiences which appear before persons as surprise or as departures from the norm.

Surprise and departures from the norm are characteristic of contemporary physics.

There are physicists who have chosen to respond enthusiastically to the subtle nuances of new meanings, even when these nuances have led the physicists into domains of thought that were completely new and that left the physicists vulnerable to the implications of the novel domains in which they found themselves.

Those physicists who have responded to the surprises within scientific experiences represent the paradigm of how to interrelate with traces of the Presence within experience. They have chosen to live vulnerably before the consequences of the surprise experiences within their research. This choice has required them to surrender the certitude and the determinism that they had relied upon in classical Newtonian physics, and to accept the apparently spontaneous and random occurrences that contemporary physics, especially quantum physics, identifies as the marks of the physical world.

Moreover, in responding to their experiences according to this New Testament criterion for acknowledging the Presence, these scientists appear to have uncovered that Presence to be within the physical world. They confirm, perhaps unknowingly, the proclamation of the New Testament–namely, that the Presence is everywhere with no exceptions.

The Presence of the New Testament is to be expected in the midst of total surprise; the parable of the Sower so characterized the Presence among persons. Consequently, the Presence is identified with the reversal of expectations, e.g., the parable of the good Samaritan.

Further, the Presence is identified with the sudden appearance of actions which seem to have no apparent analytical motive: the parable of the workers in the vineyard.

The "New Presence in the World" has been demonstrated to have a physical foundation in "Albert Einstein & Special Relativity."[4] Special relativity physics had proposed a perspective of the world that is in harmony with the world view that had been proposed by the New Testament's proclamation of the kingdom of God.

Special relativity had refashioned the classical world-view in its proposal that every physical occurrence within the world has that valid interpretation and that consequent valid meaning which is observable from a particular, but optional, point of reference. The consequence of this proposal is that the physical occurrences within the world reveal meanings to persons at one point of reference that those at a different reference point cannot observe.

The implication of that reformulation for the Presence is that those persons who have indeed glimpsed evidences of traces for the Presence in the world have interpreted the meaning that is valid from their reference point. Though their perspective cannot be judged to be a universal or absolute perspective, neither is any other perspective so to be considered to be universal or absolute.

However, there have been acutely sensitive persons who have glimpsed traces of the Presence. In the twentieth century there have been three such notable persons who have been outside of the Christian tradition: the poet Robert Bolt, the philosopher Albert Camus, and holocaust victim Anne Frank. Their consciousness of the numinous hints of the Presence within their experience illustrates the validity of Karl Rahner's phenomenology of the Presence within human consciousness.[5]

Others, such as Mother Teresa of Calcutta and Jean Vanier of Trosly-Breuil, France, have used the New Testament's criteria to discern the Presence within the world. These persons occupy, indeed, a particular point of reference. From their vantage point they have confirmed the validity of glimpses of the Presence by great religious figures such as Moses, David, Isaiah, Jeremiah, Jesus, and Paul. With the criteria of the New Testament or the phenomenology of experience fashioned by Karl Rahner[6] other contemporary religious thinkers continue to discover similar traces. Those who have written on the Presence in terms of grace come to mind, e.g., Roger Haight, Jean-Marc Laporte, David Tracy, and Leo O'Donovan.

Quantum physics has also confirmed the Presence as harmonious with modern western culture. The study of occurrences within the minute dimensions of the subatomic particles has discovered that there are most extraordinary dynamics operating within the physical world. These subatomic occurrences have summoned quantum physicists, as general relativity had summoned relativity physicists, to revise their world-view: the dynamics in the quantum world are radically different from the classically determined dynamics within the world of sense experience. Quantum physicists, like relativity physicists, have been challenged to accept the consequences of so revising their world-view. They too have been summoned to accept the vulnerability that follows upon reformulating the meaning of the world's physical occurrences. The subatomic world can be described only by rejecting the assumptions of determinism, the continuity of matter, the absolute law of local causality, and the predictive power of technology to control matter. In place of such assumptions, quantum physics has found that it must assume the occurrences within the micro-world to lack both determinism and objectivity. It has to describe these as spontaneous, i.e., that there are occurrences which appear to be uncaused. Thus, quantum physics has been able to describe these occurrences only with probability measurements, not with the certain and objective measurements of classical physics. It has discovered that the objects which appear to be material are discrete packets of energy which are constituted fundamentally by fields. It found that it could describe the occurrences in that world as caused by events that are removed by great distances from their effects. It had to acknowledge that science is unable to exercise the predictive control over matter that classical physics teaches. Moreover, it has been confronted by the apparent dualism of elementary particles, i.e., that particles behave both in wave-like and in particle-like manners.

Thus, quantum physics allows subatomic physicists to describe the micro-world only by dismissing the validity of sense experience as the criterion for meaning.[7]

Such drastic revisions in the interpretation of the fundamentals of the physical world are clearly in harmony with the proclamation by the New Testament of the Presence. The dynamics of the Presence had been there proclaimed to be personally spontaneous, not determined; to be basically not matter, but spirit; and to be not able to be predicted, but to be the consequence of the gratuitous actions of the Presence.

Thus, quantum physics, like relativity physics, has discovered in the subatomic world just those criteria of traces of the Presence that the New Testament had identified as the criteria of the divine activity within the world. Twentieth century science has, consequently, yet further demonstrated that belief in the Presence within the world is in harmony with the description of the world as discovered by modern physics.

This is not to claim that contemporary physics has demonstrated evidence of the Presence within the world, but that those who are open-minded believers in the Christian tradition and who respect modern physics can hold their belief while remaining in harmony with the scientific culture of the twentieth century. Physics has demonstrated that, as the New Testament proclaims, there are dynamics within the world that are not accessible to sense experience, that a Christian belief which is disposed to seek for traces of a Presence that is beyond the range of sense experience does not conflict with the evidence of physics. On the contrary, such a search can be considered to be a melodious counterpoint to the movements orchestrated by modern physics.

Modern Western culture has given birth to persons who are more tough-minded than tender-minded. Their toughening temperament is disposed to interpret critically all conscious experience; they therefore seek to criticize the tender-minded New Testament idealism with empirical skepticism. These persons demand that the idealistic proclamation of the Presence be submitted to the criteria of empirical science. Only with such an approach will the tough-minded be willing to consider how the Presence can modify the meaning of being human. They can be tough-minded enough to demand that the method of discovering the validity of the proclamation of the Presence is the method of the empiricism of the physical sciences. Thus, the tough-minded could have assumed that they were incapable of making sense of the tender-minded New Testament's proclamation that the kingdom of God is within the physical world.

The tender-minded, idealistic claim by New Testament scripture scholars that the kingdom of God was the core of Jesus' ministry and the theme of his own proclamation had not convinced these critically minded persons. The tough-minded person must be skeptical about an idealistic and optimistic proclamation that the spirit of God is active within every person's consciousness. Such an assertion appears to have little respect for scientific data; it appears to have lost contact with the concrete parts of life.

This tough-minded skepticism can be interpreted to be partially the consequence of the influence of positivism, which assumes that the world envisioned by sense experience is a mirror image of the world envisioned by the empiricism of physical science.

Moreover, because the kingdom of God does not appear within the battery of sense impressions, the positivist concludes that the kingdom of God clashes with the world-view of physical science, i.e., with the scientific knowledge of the physical world.

The tough-minded positivist claims to rely only upon the world-view that modern physical science has fashioned with the rigor and precision that are employed in the scientific disciplines.

Therefore a dialectical discussion between the proclamation of the kingdom and contemporary physics appeared appropriate. The purpose of this dialectic was to determine whether the world envisioned by relativity physics and quantum physics tolerates that vision of the world which includes the Presence. The intention was to derive from a scientific loyalty to the data of the physical world a more tough-minded examination of whether and how persons can intelligently reflect upon the relationship between the Presence and the world. Without such a tempering of the New Testament's proclamation, the Presence might appear to be nothing more than the kind of a vision that appears to a person during sleep-walking. Therefore, the turn to contemporary physics was expected to temper the tender-minded idealism of the New Testament with the tough-minded pragmatism of physics.

However, the contrary was the result. The turn to contemporary physics has revealed that the world-view of modern physics is in harmony with the world-view implied by the New Testament's proclamation of the Presence. Thus, the vision of the Presence within all experience has been supported by the tough-minded.

Such a refining of the vision of the Presence in the world permits the religious vision to be pragmatically maintained. That vision has appeared to be in balance with physics' intimacy with empirical data.[8]

The scientific world-view has been discovered to be vastly different from the world as envisioned by those more tender-minded persons who rely only upon the ideology fashioned from the common-sense empiricism of the senses.

The world-view of contemporary physics includes perspectives, natural forces, dynamics, and occurrences that conflict not with the proclamation of the kingdom, but with the common sense empiricism of sense experience. In fact, the world-view of twentieth century physics is far removed not from the perspective that acknowledges the kingdom, but from common-sense experience. Contemporary physics, in the effort to communicate its comprehension of the physical world, has been forced to develop a symbolic description of the natural world—a description in terms of sense experience would be at odds with the exclusively symbolic events studied by contemporary physics.

Thus, those persons who might have assumed that the proclamation of the kingdom was in conflict with the world-view of twentieth century science have discovered in this dialectic with physics that the kingdom is not in dissonance but in harmony with the modern scientific world-view. The kingdom is a coherent occurrence for those who tough-mindedly accept the perspective of contemporary physics. Conversely, the world-view of modern physics is a shock for those who insist only upon the perspective of common sense.

Thus, persons who respect the world as comprehended by relativity physics and quantum physics find that they are able intelligently to attend to the proclamation of the kingdom; they can put aside the skepticism that they might initially have assumed. They can draw inferences for faith from the scientific demonstration of unimaginable physical presences within the world: there could indeed be a Presence that explains the responses to the world of such well received persons as Moses, Jesus of Nazareth, Paul of Tarsus, Albert Camus, Anne Frank, and Robert Bolt.

There may conceivably be a divine spirit who is dynamic within every consciousness, even if this dynamic is as hidden as the quantum dynamics of the physical world. The tough-minded will be more disposed to consider that spirit to be actual than to dismiss it. They have discovered that the proclamation of the Presence is in harmony with the world as envisioned by the precision of scientific rigor.

Notes

....

Introduction

[1]Thomas Aquinas, *Summa Theologica*, 1, 1, 8.
[2]Erivin Lazlo, *The Systems View of the World*, pp. 11–12.
[3]Ibid., pp. 12–13.
[4]Ibid., p. 19.
[5]Ibid., p. 79.

Chapter 1

[1]Albert Einstein, *Albert Einstein: Philosopher–Scientist* (quoted in Page 15, *The Cosmic Code*, p. 20).
[2]Heinz Pagels, *The Cosmic Code*, pp. 20–24.
[3]Albert Einstein, "Autobiographical Notes," in *Albert Einstein: Philosopher–Scientist*, (quoted in Page 1, *The Cosmic Code*, pp. 21–22).
[4]Albert Einstein, *Relativity*, pp. 9–10.
[5]George Gamow, *Mr. Thompkins*, p. 40.
[6]Gary Zukav, *The Dancing*, pp. 165–166, 169.
[7]Ibid., pp. 170–179.
[8]Richard T. Weidner & Robert L. Sells, *Elementary Modern Physics*, pp. 17–28.
[9]Ibid., pp. 3, 17.
[10]Eric Rogers, *Physics for the Inquiring Mind*, pp. 483–484.
[11]David Halliday and Robert Resnick, *Fundamentals of Physics*, p. 124.
[12]Gary Zukav, *The Dancing*, pp. 179–180.
[13]Albert Einstein, *Relativity*, pp. 12–15.
[14]Ibid., pp. 17, 19, 20.
[15]George Gamow, *Mr. Thompkins*, pp. 63–64.
[16]Ibid., pp. 64–65.

[17]Ibid., p. ix.
[18]Ibid., pp. 55–58.
[19]Ibid., p. 62.
[20]Aristotle, *Metaphysics,* 1005b 19–20.

Chapter 2

[1]Heinz Pagels, *The Cosmic Code,* p. 41.
[2]Peter Garbiel Bergman, *Introduction to the Theory of Relativity,* pp. 156–157.
[3]Ibid., pp. 159–160.
[4]Albert Einstein, cited in Heinz Pagels, *The Cosmic Code,* p. 43.
[5]Michael Berry, *Principles of Cosmology and Gravitation,* pp. 67, 71.
[6]Ibid., p. 103.
[7]Ibid., p. 105.
[8]George Gamow, *Mr. Thompkins,* pp. 66, 67, 69, 70.
[9]Heinz Pagels, *The Cosmic Code,* pp. 49–50.
[10]Gary Zukav, *The Dancing Wu Li,* pp. 200–204.
[11]George Gamow, *Mr. Thompkins,* pp. 77–78.
[12]Ibid., pp. 189–200.
[13]Ibid., pp. 9ff.
[14]Karl Rahner, "The Experience of Grace," *A Rahner Reader,* pp. 197–198.
[15]Albert Camus, *Resistance, Rebellion, and Death,* pp. 3–8.
[16]Robert Bolt, *A Man for All Season,* preface, p. xiii.
[17]Ibid.
[18]Ibid., p. 141.
[19]Albert Einstein, quoted in Heinz Pagels, *The Cosmic Code,* pp. 55–57.
[20]Albert Einstein and Leopold Infeld, *The Evolution of Physics,* p. 152.
[21]Albert Einstein, cited in Heinz Pagels, *The Cosmic Code,* pp. 331–334.
[22]Gary Zukav, *The Dancing Wu Li,* p. 211.
[23]Ibid., pp. 141–142.

Chapter 3

[1]Louis DeBroglie, *New Perspectives in Physics,* p. 86.
[2]Gary Zukav, *The Dancing,* pp. 73, 76.

[3]Heinz Pagels, *The Cosmic Code,* pp. 25–26.
[4]Ibid., pp. 66–68.
[5]Ibid., p. 70.
[6]Ibid., p. 72.
[7]Ibid., pp. 74–77.
[8]Ibid., pp. 78–80.
[9]Ibid., pp. 81–83.
[10]Ibid., pp. 85–94.
[11]Ibid., pp. 94–95.
[12]Max Planck, *The Universe,* p. 8.
[13]Ibid., p. 14.
[14]Halliday and Resnick, *Fundamentals of Physics,* pp. 95, 777, 778.
[15]Ibid., pp. 808–810.
[16]Weidner and Sells, *Elementary Modern Physics,* pp. 89–90, 93.
[17]Halliday and Resnick, *Fundamentals of Physics,* pp. 777–778.
[18]Victor F. Weisskopf, *Knowledge and Wonder,* pp. 84–86.
[19]Gary Zukav, *The Dancing,* pp. 91–100.
[20]Ibid., pp. 51–52.
[21]Ibid., pp. 53, 56, 57.
[22]Ibid., p. 72.
[23]George Gamow, *Mr. Thompkins,* pp. 81–82.
[24]Victor Weisskopf, *Knowledge and Wonder,* pp. 96–97.
[25]George Gamow, *Mr. Thompkins,* pp. 32–33.
[26]Gary Zukav, *The Dancing,* p. 219.
[27]Ibid., p. 220.
[28]Victor Weisskopf, *Knowledge,* pp. 90–92.
[29]Heinz Pagels, *The Cosmic Code,* p. 79.
[30]Victor Weisskopf, *Knowledge,* pp. 106–107.
[31]Ibid., pp. 108–109.
[32]Heinz Pagels, *The Cosmic Code,* pp. 136, 142.
[33]Werner Heisenberg, *Physics and Philosophy,* p. 58.
[34]Victor Weisskopf, *Knowledge,* pp. 102–105.
[35]Weidner and Sells, *Elementary Modern Physics,* p. 133.
[36]Heinz Pagels, *The Cosmic Code,* pp. 265–269.
[37]Ibid., pp. 270–272.
[38]Ibid., p. 218.
[39]Ibid., pp. 219–220.
[40]Ibid., pp. 226–232, 237.
[41]Gary Zukav, *The Dancing,* pp. 255–257.
[42]Heinz Pagels, *The Cosmic Code,* pp. 234–235.
[43]Ibid., pp. 240–41, 245, 249, 251.
[44]Ibid., pp. 64ff.
[45]Ibid., pp. 144–145.

[46]Ibid., pp. 150–151.
[47]Ibid., pp. 163–164.

Chapter 4

[1]Norman Perrin, *Jesus and the Language of the Kingdom,* pp. 33–34.
[2]Augustine, *The City of God,* xvi.
[3]Norman Perrin, *Jesus and the Language,* pp. 63–64.
[4]Ibid., pp. 67–68.
[5]Ibid., pp. 159–160.
[6]*Gospel of Thomas* (81:24–82:3).
[7]Norman Perrin, *Jesus and the Language,* p. 162.
[8]Dan Otto Via, Jr., *The Parables: Literary and Existential* (Fortress, 1967) and John Dominic Crossan, *In Parables: Challenge of the Historical Jesus* (Harper & Row, 1973).
[9]Norman Perrin, *Jesus and the Language,* p. 168.
[10]Ibid., p. 195.

Chapter 5

[1]Whittaker Chambers, *Witness.*
[2]Immanuel Kant, *The Critique of Judgment.*
[3]David Hume, *An Inquiry Concerning Human Understanding.*
[4]Georg W. F. Hegel, *The Phenomenology of Mind.*
[5]Charles Sanders Peirce, *Philosophical Writings of Peirce.*
[6]Edmund Husserl, *Logical Investigations.*
[7]David Tracy, *The Analogical Imagination.*

Chapter 6

[1]William James, "The Present Dilemma," pp. 11–13.
[2]Chapter I.
[3]Chapter II.
[4]Chapter I.
[5]Chapter III (cf Karl Rahner's interpretation of human consciousness).
[6]Ibid.
[7]Chapter III.
[8]William James, "The Present Dilemma," pp. 20–23.

Bibliography

....

Books

Aristotle, *Metaphysics,* edited and translated by W. D. Ross, Oxford: The Clarendon Press, 1966.

Augustine of Hippo, *The City of God,* translated by Marcus Dods, New York: Random House, 1950.

Balthasar, Hans Urs von, *A Theological Anthropology,* New York: Sheed and Ward, 1967.

Barret, William, *The Illusion of Technique,* Garden City: Anchor Press/Doubleday, 1978.

Barbour, Ian G., *Issues in Science and Religion,* Englewood Cliffs: Prentice-Hall, 1966.

Barbour, Ian G., *Science and Religion,* New Perspectives on the Dialogue, New York: Harper & Row, 1968.

Berry, Michael, *Principles of Cosmology and Gravitation,* Cambridge: Cambridge University Press, 1976.

Bolt, Robert, *A Man for all Seasons,* A Play in Two Acts, New York: Random House, 1960.

Camus, Albert, *Resistance, Rebellion, and Death,* translated from the French by Justin O'Brien, New York: The Modern Library, 1960.

Chambers, Whittaker, *Witness,* New York: Random House, 1952.

De Broglie, Louis, *New Perspectives in Physics,* translated by A. J. Pomerans, New York: Basic Books, Inc., 1962.

Einstein, Albert, *Relativity,* The Special and the General Theory, translated by Robert W. Lawson, London: Methuen & Co., Inc., 1946.

Gamow, George, *Mr. Thompkins in Wonderland,* Cambridge, England: The University Press, 1953.

Gullaumont, A., C. Puech, G. Quispel, W. Till, and Yassah 'Abd al Masih (editors & translators), *The Gospel According to Thomas,* Leiden: E. J. Brill, 1959.

Halliday, David, and Robert Resnick, *Fundamentals of Physics,* New York: John Wiley & Son, 1981.

Hegel, Georg W. F., *The Phenomenology of Mind.* New York: The Macmillan Co., 1931.

Hume, David, *An Inquiry Concerning Human Understanding,* Oxford: Clarendon Press, 1963.

Husserl, Edmund, *Logical Investigations,* two volumes, New York: Humanities Press, 1970.

Kant, Immanuel, *The Critique of Judgment,* New York: Hafner, 1951.

Laszlo, Erwin, *The Systems View of the World,* the Natural Philosophy of the New Developments in the Sciences, New York: George Braziller, 1972.

Pagels, Heinz R., *The Cosmic Code,* Quantum Physics as the Language of Nature, New York: Simon & Schuster, 1982.

Peirce, Charles Sanders, *Philosophical Writings of Peirce,* ed. Justus Buchler, New York: Dover Publications, 1955.

Perrin, Norman, *Jesus and the Language of the Kingdom,* Symbol and Metaphor in New Testament Interpretation, Philadelphia: Fortress Press, 1976.

Planck, Max, *The Universe in the Light of Modern Physics,* translated by W. H. Johnston, London: George Allen & Unwin, Ltd., 1931.

Rahner, Karl, *A Rahner Reader,* edited by Gerald A. McCool, New York: Seabury, 1975.

Rahner, Karl & Herbert Vorgrimler, *Theological Dictionary,* edited by Cornelius Ernst, O.P., translated by Richard Strachan, New York: Herder and Herder, 1965.

Rogers, Eric M., *Physics for the Inquiring Mind,* The Methods, Nature, and Philosophy of Physical Science, Princeton: Princeton University Press, 1960.

Schillebeeckx, Edward, "God's Rule Directed at Mankind: The Kingdom of God," *Jesus,* An Experiment in Christology, trans. William Collins Sons & Co. Ltd., pp. 141–200, New York: The Seabury Press, 1979.

Toulmin, Stephen, *The Return to Cosmology,* Postmodern Science and the Theology of Nature, Berkeley and Los Angeles: University of California Press, 1982.

Tracy, David, *The Analogical Imagination,* New York: Crossroad, 1981.

Weidner, Richard T., & Robert L. Sells, *Elementary Modern Physics,* Boston: Allyn and Bacon, Inc., 1980.

Weisskopf, Victor F., *Knowledge and Wonder,* The Natural World as Man Knows It, Garden City: Doubleday & Co., Inc., 1962.

Wilson, J. R. S., *Emotion and Object,* Cambridge: The University Press, 1972.

Zukav, Gary, *The Dancing Wu Li Masters,* An Overview of the New Physics, New York: William Morrow and Company, Inc., 1979.

Articles

Adler, Dr. Mortimer, J., "Positivism or Science," Institute of Technology of Wright–Patternson Air Base; Dayton, Ohio, January 21, 1960.

Byrne, Patrick H., "Lonergan on the Foundations of the Theories of Relativity," *Creativity and Method: Essays in Honor of Bernard Lonergan, S. J.,* ed. Matthew L. Lamb, pp. 477–494, Milwaukee: Marquette University Press, 1981.

Duling, Dennis, "Norman Perrin and the Kingdom of God: Review and Response," *Journal of Religion,* 1984.

Goss, James, "Eschatology, Autonomy, and Individuation: The Evocative Power of the Kingdom," *Journal of the American Academy of Religion,* vol. XLIX, no. 3, Sept. 1981, pp. 363–381.

Greeley, Andrew M., "Sociology and Theology: Some Methodological Questions," *Proceedings of the Catholic Theological Society of America* June 12–15, 1977, vol. 32, pp. 31–54.

Hodgson, Peter, "Implications of Quantum Physics I–III," *The Month,* July/August 1984, pp. 219–222; September 1984, pp. 296–299; July/August 1985, pp. 256–258.

Holton, Gerald, "Einstein, Michelson, and the 'Crucial' Experiment," *Isis,* vol. 60, 2, no. 202, 1969, pp. 133–197.

James, William, "The Present Dilemma in Philosophy," *Pragmatism* (Cambridge: Harvard University Press, 1975), pp. 9–26.

Tracy, David, "Presidential Address," *Proceedings of the Catholic Theological Society of America* June 12–15, 1977, vol. 32, pp. 234–244.

Tracy, David, "Grace and the Search for the Human: The Sense of the Uncanny," *Proceedings of the Catholic Theological Society of America* June 13–16, 1979, vol. 34, pp. 64–77.

Index